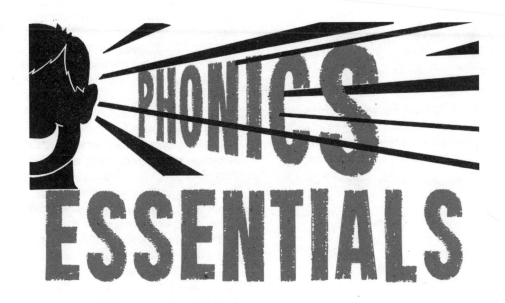

PHONICS ESSENTIALS

Gill Budgell

theguardian
teachernetwork
teachers.guardian.co.uk

RISING ★ STARS

Rising Stars UK Ltd, 7 Hatchers Mews, Bermondsey Street, London SE1 3GS
www.risingstars-uk.com

Published 2012
Text, design and layout © Rising Stars UK Ltd.

Editorial: Dawn Booth

Design: Words & Pictures Ltd, London

Cover Design: Mark Ecob

The publishers and author would like to thank the following for permission to use copyright material.

p.7 Gill Budgell and Kate Ruttle, *Penpals for Handwriting Year 1 Teacher's Book* (2003), Cambridge University Press, reproduced with permission; p.18 Cheeky Chimps Magnetic Letters available from TTS Group; p.18 Read Write Inc. Phonics Green Word Cards by Ruth Miskin, Oxford University Press, reproduced with permission; p.18 Check and Progress Phonics Cards (2012), Louise Glasspoole. © Rising Stars UK Ltd; p.18 Decodable Ping-pong Balls available from TTS Group; p.25 Oxford Reading Tree Floppy's Phonics: Sounds and Letters: Frieze, Oxford University Press, reproduced with permission; p.25 Phonics Flashcards, Oxford University Press, reproduced with permission; p.27 Robin Phinizy/iStockphoto; p.32 Phoneme Fan available from TTS Group; p.32 Phoneme Fan parts. Image courtesy of Free Early Years Resource website, www.earlylearninghq.org.uk; p.32 Whopper Phonic Worm from Sweet Counter; p.35 Sintez/iStockphoto; p.58 Learning Resources Phonics Bean Bags, Learning Resources Magnet Letter Board and Learning Resources Dice, www.LearningResources.co.uk; p.63 Thrass Phoneme Machine program, www.thrass.co.uk; p.67 Text from Reading Rockets' website, www.readingrockets.org; p.67 Dmitriy Kalinin/iStockphoto; p.70 Reproduced from *Very First Reading: Dog Diaries* by permission of Usborne Publishing, 83–85 Saffron Hill, London EC1N 8RT, UK. www.usborne.com. © 2010 Usborne Publishing Ltd; p.71 Practice Book from Get Reading Right, www.getreadingright.co.uk; p.71 Check and Progress Phonics Cards (2012), Louise Glasspoole. © Rising Stars UK Ltd; p.71 Decoding and Comprehension Posters from Prim-Ed Publishing; p.76 Ruth Miskin, Read Write Inc. *Phonics Handbook*, 2011, Oxford University Press, reproduced with permission; p.78 Phonics Phase 5 Magnetic Letters from TTS Group; p.86 trugs from Read Successfully, www.readsuccessfully.com; p.86 Phonicshark by White Space, www.wordshark.co.uk; p.89 Various series for the older learner © Rising Stars UK Ltd; p.89 Front covers of Project X CODE *The Adventure Begins*, Oxford University Press, reproduced with permission; p.89 Rapid Phonics series from Pearson. Reproduced with permission; p.104 *Phonics Check and Progress*, by Louise Glasspoole, 2012. © Rising Stars UK Ltd; p.105 *Phonics & Early Reading Assessment for Reception* (PERA), by Colin McCarty & Kate Ruttle, 2012. Reproduced by permission of Hodder Education; p.105 *Diagnostic Test of Word Reading Processes* © Institute of Education, University of London, 2012. Reproduced by permission of GL Assessment Ltd; p.113 Top: www.educationcity.com; p.113 Bottom: Iwona Grodzka/iStockphoto; p.114 Roxana Gonzalez/iStockphoto; p.116 Phonics Outdoor Signs and Outdoor High-Frequency signs available from TTS Group; pp.117–119 *Dockside Starters: Stage 1 Teacher's Book* © Rising Stars UK Ltd.

British Library Cataloguing-in-Publication Data.

A CIP record for this book is available from the British Library.

ISBN: 978-0-85769-411-9

Printed by Ashford Colour Press

FSC
www.fsc.org
MIX
Paper from responsible sources
FSC® C011748

CONTENTS

When I run training sessions with teachers, I often begin with this question – how many ways can you spell *phonics*?

After much hushed and often quite intense collaboration, we produce a slide that looks something like the one on the right.

We can produce this number of spellings because we are literate and understand the rules of the **alphabetic code**.

Actually, we don't obey all the rules, since words in English never begin with the letters ff, but there are always 'creatives' in the audience.

foniks
ffoniks
phonnichs phonicks
phonix fonicks ffonix phonics ffonichs phonix fonix
fonichs phonichs

However, this exercise provides a snapshot of what phonics is – owning and understanding a bank of knowledge about how letters and sounds work in English and using it for a range of purposes.

We might then continue with an exploration of this word …

GHOTI

What is 'GHOTI', what does it say, who wrote it and why? Attributed to George Bernard Shaw, this word could feasibly spell the word *fish*, re-spelled to demonstrate the inconsistency of English spelling: **gh** as in *cough*, **o** as in *women*, **ti** as in *nation*.

So, we understand that the English alphabetic code consists of letter shapes that, in various combinations, form a code for about 44 speech sounds.

GREEK – PHŌNĒMA
'A SOUND UTTERED'

Some languages have an exact match in their code so the number of letters matches the number of sounds. But English is tricky because the 26 letter shapes must be used in various combinations (they even double up – think of the two pronunciations of **ow**, for example) to make about 44 sounds. It's tricky.

Alphabetic principle

English	Spanish
Deep orthography	Shallow orthography
40+ spoken sounds represented by 26 letters (and no accents)	Number of letter sounds = Number of letter patterns

What of politics?

> Learn to read so that we can read to learn.
> Nick Gibb

Michael Gove and Nick Gibb are ministers with a passion for phonics. They have pushed the boundaries of government to ensure that all teachers teach systematic **synthetic phonics** to all children. Sir Jim Rose comments that this is new territory in recent history; governments usually specify the 'how' not 'what'.

> Methodology is not normally specified. Phonics is not just a method. It's not optional. It's content. Its goal is comprehension.
> Sir Jim Rose

> There is more to reading than phonics. But high-quality evidence from across the world – from Scotland and Australia to the National Reading Panel in the US – shows that the systematic teaching of synthetic phonics is the best way to teach literacy to all children, and especially those aged 5–7 years.
> Michael Gove

We find Ofsted inspectors undertaking training in early reading skills in order to be able to assess best practice and we find a new Phonics Screening Check for all 6-year-olds to ensure that no child slips through the net. We find the equivalent of a BOGOFF (buy one, get one free) deal available for purchasing phonic resources and training that has been quality assured by a panel of phonic experts.

> In November 2010, the UK government's Schools White Paper, *The Importance of Teaching* (available from www.education.gov.uk/publications/)stated its case for phonics, saying that it would: *Ensure that all children have the chance to follow an enriching curriculum by getting them reading early. That means supporting the teaching of systematic synthetic phonics and introducing a simple reading check at age six to guarantee that children have mastered the basic skills of early reading and also ensure we identify those with learning difficulties.*
>
> *The Importance of Teaching*, DfE, 2010, para. 4.6

And what of previous methods?

We used to teach 'look and say' where the children were encouraged to use memory and other visual clues as well as rhyme and analogy. And for high-frequency **tricky words** we encouraged a range of strategies too: just remember it; look at its first/last letter; look at its shape; or associate a picture with it as a **mnemonic**.

Analytic phonics was the approach first adopted by the National Literacy Strategy when it was introduced in 1998.

> **Basics – analytic phonics**
> Reading or writing **dog**   –   **d-og**
> Means you can read or write   –   **d-ig, d-ip, d-ot**
> Or   –   **d-og, f-og, fr-og, b-og**

And synthetic phonics?

Synthetic phonics explicitly teaches children how to crack the alphabetic code. We don't rely on guesswork.

> Reading **cat**
>   /c/ /a/ /t/
> - Three letters.
> - Three pure sounds.
> - Blend the sounds.
> - Read the word.
>
> Writing **dog**
> - Say the word.
> - Segment it into **phonemes** /d/ /o/ /g/.
> - Say them in turn.
> - Write a letter for each sound to write the word.

The research evidence for one method being clearly better than another is simply not available, but in its absence it is better to proceed with a systematic teaching model rather than an unsystematic model or no phonics teaching at all. So the principles of high-quality phonic work were drafted for the teaching profession.

So what makes an effective phonics programme?

1. Set within a broad and balanced curriculum.
2. Systematic – with a clearly defined and structured progression.
3. Discrete daily lesson delivered at pace.
4. Underpinned by a synthetic phonics approach.
5. Teaches **segmenting** and **blending** as reverse processes.
6. Uses a multi-sensory approach.
7. Promotes speaking and listening as the foundation for embarking on phonics.
8. Provides clear guidance on how to assess progress to inform the next steps.
9. Offers guidance about adapting the programme for special needs.

Phonics is a means to an end; we aim for automatic word recognition **comprehension**.

This book is an *Essentials* book about phonics; it cannot be comprehensive but offers links where space on the page has limited the amount of information possible. It touches on the essential issues, knowledge and skills for adults who are interested in teaching reading with a sense of today's expectations.

CHAPTER 1 THE BIG IDEA: THE ALPHABETIC CODE

The alphabet

TOP TIP

The alphabet is not the same as the **alphabetic code**. Make sure you know and understand this very important distinction!

The alphabet in English has 26 letters which we teach to children with an emphasis on letter formation. We teach both lower-case and upper-case, or capital, forms of each letter.

Many schools adopt different styles which have differing letter formation. For example, some prefer letters with loops, some with exit flicks, some with entry strokes. The following show a variety of different styles:

y ч y Y y ȳ̱ ʯ ʸ y ʼY ʯ Y

Only six of the letters are the same in lower-case and upper-case forms: Cc, Oo, Ss, Vv, Xx, Zz. So once you've chosen a handwriting style you are happy to adopt, teach it consistently and teach the remaining 20 pairs of letters. Some organisations suggest that it is helpful to teach joined writing (and so letters with loops) from the very beginning of learning. However, it is more common to teach letters with an exit flick. This finishes the letter off, but in a way that leads naturally to joined writing at a later stage. Check out the National Handwriting Association website (www.nha-handwriting.org.uk/) for more information.

The children will see varying letter forms and fonts in the environment, but for teaching purposes consistency is very important. Be sure to select your chosen handwriting resource or style and ensure that it is taught across the whole school.

The children need to be taught that lower case and upper case represent the same letter name and letter sound. The children in Spain learn their language in upper case, so it is a UK peculiarity that we focus so heavily on lower case when it is important to know and understand both letter forms.

Alphabet posters help to reinforce letter formation, like the one shown here from Gill Budgell and Kate Ruttle's *Penpals for Handwriting Year 1 Practice Book* (Cambridge University Press, 2003), and alphabet songs are useful for saying the letter sounds and names (as well as being fun for general language development, sense of rhythm, rhyme, etc.).

a b c d e f g h i j k l m n
o p q r s t u v w x y z
A B C D E F G H I J K L
M N O P Q R S T U V W
X Y Z

Alphabet poster from *Penpals for Handwriting Year 1 Practice Book.*

Alphabetical order becomes important over time for dictionary work or tasks that require alphabetical sorting.

However, it's important to only use *letter sounds* for oral **blending** (saying the letter sounds and blending them together until you can begin to hear the word emerging) and **segmenting** (splitting the sounds within a word as you say it, so that you can identify the different sounds in a word in order to spell it), and also for reading and spelling in the early stages.

Most **synthetic phonic** schemes avoid letter names completely in the early stages of the programme. The Department for Education (DfE) programme, *Letters and Sounds*, suggests introducing letter names in Phase 3 towards the end of Reception.

> **TOP TIP**
>
> There are many alphabetic code charts now available online, often as part of synthetic phonics programmes. Search for 'alphabetic code charts' and you will see various options.

The alphabetic code

The alphabetic code helps us to understand the relationship between the sounds in our speech and what we actually write to represent those sounds. The idea is simple, but in English the application is quite complex. Look at the following chart:

Fact There are in the region of 44 sounds in our spoken language.

> Challenge! Create 44 sounds from 26 letters.

Fact But there are only 26 written letter forms, i.e. the alphabet.

Fact We have to use combinations of the 26 letters to make the 44 sounds.

> We have about 176 spellings for the 44 sounds. Rather than allocating one discrete combination for each sound, we complicate matters by having several options available for many of the sounds. There are often several ways to write the same sound and there are often several ways to pronounce the same letters.

A good chart will show at least two levels of alphabetic code:

⭐ Simple: one letter to represent one sound, e.g. **m** for sound /**m**/ or **s** for sound /s/ and some two-letter sound exemplars, e.g. **ch**, **sh**.

⭐ Complex: all other combinations, in which two, three or even four letters are used to represent one sound, e.g. **ch**, **air**, **ough**, as well as the notion that different letters can represent the same sound, e.g. **e** in *bed*, **ea** in *bread*, **ai** in *said*, **a** in *any* and **u** in *bury* can all represent the sound /e/.

The children need to understand all of the simple code quite quickly, but they also need to be taught examples of the complex code from early on so that they are introduced to its key principles. Eventually the children move from understanding just one or two examples of the complex code to understanding that there are many variables available to them for reading and spelling. When they have grasped the full complexity of the English spelling code and know how to use it effectively, they will have cracked the alphabetic code.

This chapter continues to explain what the alphabetic code is. To find out more about how to teach the code see Chapters 7–10.

One letter: one sound

In most synthetic phonics programmes the simplest level of the alphabetic code is understanding that there is one letter matching one sound for 19 **consonants** and the five **vowels**:

$$b, c, d, f, g, h, j, k, l, m, n, p, r, s, t, v, w, y, z$$
$$a, e, i, o, u$$

(Note that **q** and **x** are not included in this category.)

Chapter 5 outlines the importance of teaching this simple level of code in a specific order to ensure that the children learn the sounds and can immediately recognise them and begin to blend them for their early reading. The sequence for teaching, generally in groups of four letters per week, is likely to be along the lines of:

$$s, a, t, p, i, n, m, d, g, o, c, k, ck, e, u, r, h, b, f, l, j, v, w, y, z$$

For each of these letters (and their upper-case equivalent) we teach the children one corresponding sound. The sound you say must be as pure as possible with no '**uh**' on the end. It generally means that the pronunciation is cut short.

We say: /n/ not /nuh/, /f/ not /fuh/, /k/ for letters **c**, **k** and **ck**.

For some voiced letters, such as **b, d, g, v, z, j, l, m, n, r, w** and **th** as in this) it is very difficult not to add a little /uh/ at the end, but you should consciously try to avoid this.

Note that **q** and **x** are not listed here. They are oddities because:

⭐ **q** is only ever used with **u** and therefore becomes a **digraph** (two letters). However, it also then has two sounds: /k/ and /w/. So **qu** is an example of 'two letters and two sounds'.

TOP TIP

It can be difficult to feel the difference between a voiced and voiceless or unvoiced sound. This test may help. Put a piece of paper in front of your mouth when saying the sounds – the paper should move when saying the unvoiced sounds:

p, t, k, f, s, h.

This also applies to the unvoiced sounds met in later stages: **sh** and **ch**, and **th** as in **thin**.

x is code for the sounds /k/ and /s/; it is an example of 'one letter but two sounds'. Some programmes teach that **x** and **cks** are both code for /k//s/, as in **box** and **ducks**.

 q and **x** aren't common letters but the children need to be taught why they are exceptions. Using *queue* or *x-ray* in a phonics scheme or alphabetic book is unhelpful since they stress the rather unusual case where a letter is code for its letter name. Similarly, never use *xylophone* as an example for letter **x**, since in that case the **x** is code for the sound /z/. Better to use more common examples such as *queen* or *quiz* and examples of **x** where it features commonly at the end of a word, such as in *box* or *fox*.

Two, three or four letters: one sound

The notion of two, three or four letters representing a single sound is fundamental to understanding the alphabetic code. There are simple and complex examples of this rule. Some synthetic phonics schemes and phonics experts prefer to teach the most common examples as part of the simple code. For example, they might teach **ch**, **sh**, **th**, **ng**, **ear** and the oddities **qu** and **x**, but leave **kn**, **gn** and **wh** and **ture** until later.

An alphabetic chart clearly flags examples of these letter combinations (referred to as **graphemes**) and provides example words. However, some letter combinations are more common and easier to grasp than others, so it is usual to find a sequence for gradual teaching in any synthetic phonics reading programme.

In *Letters and Sounds* and as outlined in Chapter 5 of this book, this notion is introduced at Phase 2 with **ff**, **ll** and **ss**, and with two different letters **ck**. Then in Phase 3 we continue with the oddities of **x** and **qu** as well as **zz** before progressing to 18 further two- and three-letter graphemes, each representing one sound. These are listed in the chart below.

Graphemes (letters)	Example word	Graphemes (letters)	Example word
ch	*chop*	ar	*car*
sh	*ship*	or	*for*
th	*thin/this*	ur	*fur*
ng	*sing*	ow	*cow*
ai	*rain*	oi	*coin*
ee	*bee*	ear	*near*
igh	*night*	air	*hair*
oa	*coat*	ure	*pure*
oo	*moon/book*	er	*dinner*

At this stage many synthetic phonics programmes also include:

⭐ **nk** /ngk/, e.g. *pink*　　⭐ **dge** /j/, e.g. *fudge*

⭐ **ve** /v/, e.g. *have*　　⭐ **tch** /ch/, e.g. *fetch*

TOP TIP ✍

The *schwa* is always a stressed vowel. Note the difference in sound between **er** in *herd* and **er** in *teacher*.

As well as:

⭐ having a choice of different first graphemes to represent sounds, e.g. **ay** instead of **ai**

⭐ avoiding **ure** /yoor/ as it is difficult to exemplify with simple words; or teach it alongside **ture** /ch/ as in *adventure*

⭐ teaching the other spellings of the *schwa* sound (a sound represented by a range of different letters but most closely likened to the sound /u/), as illustrated by the word *here* and by the **er** of the word *teacher* (see page 81)

⭐ flagging the issues of northern/southern pronunciation differences of words such as *book*.

The key message is that there is no right or wrong time to introduce these examples, but there must be a systematic teaching sequence to ensure incremental learning. *Letters and Sounds* or any of the DfE approved programmes will provide this.

Different letters: same sound

The notion of different letters coding for the same sound is also fundamental to understanding and cracking the alphabetic code.

An alphabetic chart clearly flags examples of these spelling combinations and provides example words. However, some letter combinations are more common and easier to grasp than others, so it is usual to find a sequence for gradual teaching in any synthetic phonics reading programme. The children will have already learned at least one spelling for each letter sound (a **phoneme**). At a simple level they may learn that **c**, **k** and **ck** all represent the sound /k/. As they progress so they will discover a whole world of spelling possibilities and they will learn how to make an informed choice.

In *Letters and Sounds* and as outlined in Chapter 5 of this book, this notion is introduced at Phase 5 with new graphemes for reading and new spellings for each phoneme. In Phase 6 letter combinations in the context of spelling rules and grammar are explored.

Typically the children will learn new graphemes for reading sounds they already know, as illustrated in the chart below.

Known graphemes	New graphemes	Example word	Example words
ai	ay	*say*	*rain spray*
	a-e	*cake*	*rainbow cake*
ee	ea	*tea*	a *bee* in *tea*
	ey	*key*	a *jeep key*
	e-e	*Steve*	*Steve* in a *jeep*
igh	ie	*tie*	*bright tie*
	i-e	*ride*	*high ride*
oa	oe	*toe*	a *toe* in the *road*
	o-e	*bone*	a *toad home*
oo	ue	*blue*	*blue moon*
	ew	*chew*	*chew* your *food*
	u-e	*rule*	*zoo rule*
w	wh	*whale*	*whale watch*
f	ph	*dolphin*	*fat dolphin*
or	aw	*yawn*	a *sort* of *yawn*
	au	*August*	*born* in *August*
ur	ir	*twirl*	*turn* and *twirl*
ow	ou	*about*	*clowning about*
oi	oy	*toy*	*toy coin*
	(y)u	*computer*	a *new computer*
	(y)ew	*new*	
	(y)u-e	*huge*	*huge rescue*
	(y)ue	*rescue*	

Try using simple paired words such as listed here to show the children how these spellings work. Then they may try to write their own.

The children will eventually need to know even more graphemes for known phonemes, such as:

a as in **apron**

ea as in **break**

eigh as in **eight**

ey as in **grey**

and even …

ae as in **sundae**.

This level of understanding is needed to master the most complex aspects of the alphabetic code.

Same letter(s): different pronunciation for reading or sound for spelling

The final fundamental lesson of the alphabetic code is that the same letters can represent different sounds for reading and/or spelling. You'll see from the following chart that there will always be unusual examples that arise. Don't be afraid to discuss these with the children if they are curious as it will not confuse them. Also, use children's names as an opportunity to tackle some challenging spellings.

They learn new ways to say graphemes they already know for reading.		They learn new spellings for phonemes they already know.	
Known graphemes	**Examples of different pronunciations**	**Known phonemes**	**Examples of different spellings**
a	*apple, wash, angel bath* (if southern pronunciation)	/ch/	*chat, catch, picture*
e	*end, she*	/j/	*jet, badge, orange, gentle/giraffe/gym*
i	*in, find*	/m/	*mum, lamb*
o	*on, go*	/n/	*net, gnat, knot*
u	*up, unit, put*	/r/	*red, write, rhino*
ow	*owl, show*	/oo/	*book, could, full*
ie	*pie, chief*	/z/	*zap, flies, please, freeze*
ea	*tea, head*	/or/	*for, paw, your, talk, taught/bought, sore*
er	*teacher, her*	/ee/	*bee, tea, me, happy, thief, key*
ou	*out, you, shoulder*	/s/	*sit, cellar, dance, listen, house*
y	*yes, by, gym, funny*	/ar/	*car, pass* (if southern pronunciation), *half*
ch	*chips school, Christmas chef*	/ear/	*hear, cheer, pier, here*
c	*cat, icy*	/air/	*hair, hare, pear, there*
g	*got, Gill*	/ur/	*fur, word, bird*
ey	*money, grey*	/u/	*but, couple, favour*
		/yoo/	*due, tune, stew, united*

Some programmes differentiate between /ch/ in *chat* and /chu/ in *picture.*

Unusual: *autumn*

Unusual: *quarter, water, war, poor*

Unusual: *sardines*

Unusual: *scissors*

Unusual: *earth, verb*

Unusual: *metre, thorough*

Unusual: *feud*

Other is a good example of **o** for /u/ at the beginning and **er** for /u/ at the end.

CHAPTER 2 SYNTHETIC AND ANALYTIC PHONICS: WHAT'S THE DIFFERENCE?

What you need to know

Phonics has become an acceptable and popular method for teaching children to read. However, there are different ways in which it is used, and disagreement over which approach is best.

There are two primary approaches to teaching phonics: analytic phonics and **synthetic phonics**.

To different extents, both approaches:

 require the child to have some **phonological awareness** (the ability to hear and discriminate sounds in spoken words)

 support the on-going development of the children's phonological awareness.

Phonological awareness is an essential skill for reading, writing, listening and speaking, but only a small part of phonological awareness is essential for phonics teaching.

Phonemic awareness: is the ability to identify, hear and work with the smallest units of sound — **phonemes**. It is a sub-category of phonological awareness but is the part that is essential for phonics teaching.

Phonological awareness: includes phonemic awareness plus the ability to hear, identify and manipulate larger units of sound such as syllables, rimes and onsets.

Most people agree that the analytic and synthetic approaches are fundamentally opposite, although both approaches are underpinned by academic research. This chapter attempts to highlight the similarities, differences and strengths of each in an unbiased way.

The current view is that whilst many aspects of analytic phonics such as letter patterns, analogy and rhyme are fun to explore as part of a broader language development programme, or later as part of a spelling programme, they play no part in a systematic phonics programme which is synthetic and supports the essential skills necessary to crack the **alphabetic code**.

Synthetic phonics involves the development of phonemic awareness from the outset. As part of the

decoding process, the reader learns up to 44 phonemes (the smallest units of sound) and their related **graphemes** (the written symbols for the phoneme).

As synthetic phonics is the current preferred and statutory method of teaching phonics, there are many gurus emerging. You may know some of these in relation to academic research or to classroom resources. Search on any of their names to find out more or visit the website for the Reading Reform Foundation: www.rrf.org.uk.

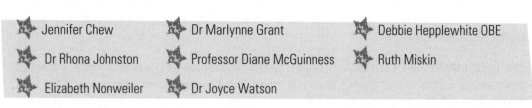

Jennifer Chew	Dr Marlynne Grant	Debbie Hepplewhite OBE
Dr Rhona Johnston	Professor Diane McGuinness	Ruth Miskin
Elizabeth Nonweiler	Dr Joyce Watson	

In contrast, analytic phonics, sometimes known as the Whole Word Approach, involves analysis of whole words to identify patterns which may be aural (hearing that **bear**, **pair**, **there** all have the /air/ sound in them) or visual (seeing that **fair**, **hair**, **lair**, **pair** all have a rime ending of **air**), then splitting them into smaller parts to help with decoding. It also assumes that having learned a pattern in one place it is possible to apply that to help decoding of other similar words when met in a different place.

There is less new or current research in the field of analytic phonics, but search on the following names for more information about studies reaching back to the late 1980s, or visit the Initial Teacher Education – English website (www.ite.org.uk) for more information.

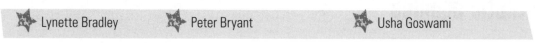

Lynette Bradley	Peter Bryant	Usha Goswami

International picture

There is international evidence to suggest that synthetic phonics is fast, efficient and effective, even with those who are more likely to find reading and spelling difficult (e.g. boys, bilingual learners and those with special learning needs).

UK

The UK made it mandatory that all state primary schools teach early reading and spelling with systematic, synthetic phonics by 2007. This arose from The Rose Report: *Independent Review of the Teaching of Early Reading*.

The UK government has supported schools to purchase approved systematic synthetic phonic resources with an unprecedented 'match-funding' programme of up to £6,000 for a limited period of time, and has committed to tackling complacency or non-compliance with refocused training for Ofsted inspectors as well as a new focus on initial teacher training institutions (ITTs). There is also a Year 1 Phonics Screening Check for all children aged 6 years to ensure that the basic phonic skills of decoding have been secured and understood in order to allow the children to continue making good progress as a reader.

Australia

Australia recommended 'an early and systematic emphasis on the explicit teaching of phonics' in the report: *The National Inquiry into the Teaching of Literacy* (2005, www.dest.gov.au/nitl/documents/report_recommendations.pdf).

The Australian National Curriculum (www.australiancurriculum.edu.au), which is being developed progressively, stipulates that phonics should be taught from Kindergarten through to Year 2 and from the simple to complex.

USA

The USA researched every major method to teach children how to read and concluded: 'systematic phonics instruction produces significant benefits for students in Kindergarten through 6th grade and for children having difficulty learning to read'.

This was reported in: *National Reading Panel Findings* (www.nationalreadingpanel.org).

Synthetic phonics

Reading with synthetic phonics involves decoding or 'breaking' words into separate phonemes which can then be blended together to read a written word. This process is called **synthesising sounds**. The process of spelling with **synthetic phonics** requires children to hear and identify the phonemes in a word and then use their knowledge of the letters associated with those phonemes to write or 'make' the word. This process is referred to as **segmenting**.

Synthetic phonics teaches children:

- how to systematically crack the alphabetic code of English
- that spoken words are composed of phonemes (sounds)
- in the region of 44 phonemes
- all the different ways each phoneme can be written
- to blend phonemes in a word to read

to listen for phonemes in words in order to write them as graphemes for spelling

 regular and irregular, **high-frequency words** which are essential for both reading and writing.

Synthetic phonics moves quickly – children are taught at least four sounds a week in the early stages.

Absolute basics of synthetic phonics

How to read the word *cat*
/c/ /a/ /t/
- Three letters.
- Three pure sounds.
- Blend the sounds.
- Read the word.

How to write the word *dog*
- Say the word.
- Segment it into phonemes /d/ /o/ /g/.
- Say them in turn.
- Write a letter for each sound to write the word.

Absolute rules of phonics

 Needs to be the prime approach to decoding text, even for words that are not completely phonically **decodable**.

 Enables the children to start learning phonic knowledge and skills using a systematic programme by the age of 5, with the expectation that they will be fluent readers by the end of Key Stage 1 (age 6).

 Is taught discretely and daily.

 Progresses from simple to more complex phonic knowledge and skills and covers the major grapheme/phoneme correspondences.

 Teaches that phonemes are blended in order, from left to right, 'all through the word' for reading.

 Teaches that words can be segmented into phonemes for spelling and that this is the reverse of **blending** phonemes to read words.

 Teaches high-frequency 'tricky' words that are not completely phonically decodable as well as those that are.

 Expects children to practice by reading texts which are entirely decodable for them at any given stage.

(Based on the DfE Core Criteria for Assessing Synthetic Phonic Resources.)

TOP TIP

What you can say

- *Let's try to hear how many sounds are in this word.*

- *Say the word, say the sounds.*

- *Show me a finger (or let's write a box/line) for each sound in the word.*

- *Let's write a letter for each sound in the word.*

- *Let's check that we have written the right sounds to make this word.*

- *Let's try to read this word – say a sound for each letter.*

- *Say the sounds faster, faster, faster – until you can hear the word. Say the word!*

A selection of synthetic phonics techniques and equipment

1. Use **sound-talk**. Say *This is my c-oa-t* as you put on your hat. The children will soon tell you that it is wrong!
2. Use sound buttons to teach blending of words:

if map snap farm

3. Use magnetic letters to build words, like the Cheeky Chimps from TTS Group.
4. Use word cards such as the Read Write Inc. Phonics Green Word Cards (Ruth Miskin, Oxford University Press): all words should be decodable and matched to the appropriate phase of teaching.
5. Use large letter or grapheme cards for the children to hold and physically organise themselves into words.
6. Use small objects with initial letter sounds to match each phoneme in tubs or bags.
7. Use a large set of dominoes that feature words and (not matching) pictures to match letter(s) to sound, in a familiar game format.
8. Use nonsense or pseudo-words to really test the children's ability to decode. Try the Check and Progress Phonics Cards (Louise Glasspoole, 2012), which are part of Check and Progress Phonics produced by Rising Stars.
9. Use captions, phrases or sentence banks – including questions and instructions that are decodable for the children.
10. Use decodable texts.

Cheeky Chimps Magnetic Letters from TTS Group.

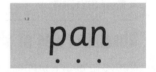

Read Write Inc. Phonics Green Word Cards by Ruth Miskin, Oxford University Press.

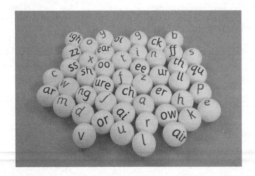

You could use ping-pong balls such as these from TTS Group.

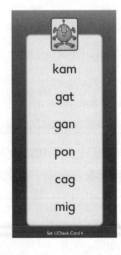

Check and Progress Phonics Cards from Rising Stars.

 Don't use pictures to make reading into a guessing game and don't use letter names in the early stages.

A note about ...

Dots, dashes and sound buttons

These are often used in programmes to help children notice the phonemes in a word. So a simple **consonant**–**vowel**–consonant (CVC) word, such as *cat* would just have three dots, but a word like *night* would have a dot under **n**, a dash (under **igh**) and a dot under **t**.

$$\underset{\bullet}{n}\,\underset{—}{igh}\,\underset{\bullet}{t}$$

Systematic synthetic phonics demands a teaching sequence that will allow children to use their knowledge in order to blend and segment from an early stage.

High-frequency and tricky words and tweaking

Systematic synthetic phonics demands a phonics first approach to even those tricky words which don't immediately seem to follow all the rules. When words have tricky bits it may be necessary to 'tweak' or adjust phonic knowledge to arrive at the word. For more about tweaking, see Chapter 3.

Decodable books

Systematic synthetic phonics demands that children practise their blending skills by reading texts that are decodable using phonic knowledge and skills. These **decodable books** have been designed and written systematically and specifically, to ensure that children can read them independently and successfully. Many new resources are now available.

The place of pictures

Systematic synthetic phonics does not allow for guessing a word from a picture or using existing knowledge in order to guess a meaning.

Rules

Systematic synthetic phonics teaches children the rules of English so they can use them to crack the code and become successful readers.

Analytic phonics

Core criteria

Reading with analytic phonics usually involves starting with whole-word sight vocabulary and reading books which can then be accessed by using a range of strategies such as a picture, initial letter or context clues. The texts provided usually have a repetitive sentence to further support the reader in guessing or predicting the words. Alphabet letter sounds are introduced slowly and some **digraphs** may be taught as they arise, with letter patterns taught later.

Analytic phonics teaches children:

- how to use a range of clues to read a text

- that knowing the initial letter of a word may help you to guess it

- both letter names and sounds from early on but either alphabetically or as they arise in materials

- to use visual memory to remember sight-words – especially if they are high-frequency tricky words

- to sound a word out as a last strategy not a first strategy

- how to use analogy to make attempts at words for reading and spelling

- reading and spelling separately.

Typically, alphabetical letters and their sounds are taught quite slowly, sometimes as few as one a week.

> **TOP TIP**
>
> Words may be analysed for patterns based on the onset (start sound) and rime (ending). For example in **strap** the **str** would be the onset and **ap** the rime. You can then go on to find other words with the same rime that will, of course, rhyme, e.g. **cap**, **tap**, **flap**.

Absolute basics of analytic phonics

How to read or write the word ***dog***.

Reading or writing ***dog***	**d-og**
Means you can read or write	**d-ig, d-ip, d-ot**
Or	**d-og, f-og, fr-og, b-og**

A selection of analytic phonics techniques and equipment

1. **Flashcards** for whole-word learning or flashcards with pictures for supporting whole-word learning.
2. Alphabet cards for learning letter names and sounds.
3. Picture and sound cards.
4. Rhyming and memory games.
5. Blend cards for snap-, lotto-type games, e.g. words beginning with **bl** as if /bl/ were one sound or **str** as if /str/ were one sound, not three.
6. Reading books in which the context and pictures support the words but which do not attempt to control the language in terms of phonemic knowledge.
7. Alphabet frieze and alphabet songs.
8. Collections of objects that feature the same initial letter or sound.

A note about ...

Sequence

Usually the teaching sequence is the alphabet, and the focus is on the 26 letters and their corresponding sounds. Sometimes **ch**, **sh**, **th** are covered but usually little of the more complex aspects of the alphabetic code such as same sound, different letters or vice versa is included.

Sounds

Sounds are often taught with a /u/ on the end, which makes blending difficult, e.g. **suh-u-nuh** rather than the pure sounds of /s//u//n/.

High-frequency and tricky words

> *the*   *said*   *some*   *when*   *people*

Analytic phonics encourages children to remember tricky words, so you may be familiar with a method called 'Look, say, cover, write, check', which essentially encourages children to memorise a spelling. The children may also be encouraged to look at the outline shape of a word (such as ***when***), or to develop **mnemonics** such as an image to prompt the memory. They would not be using phonics as a first strategy because these are words which are considered to be outside the rules – you just have to learn them!

TOP TIP

What you can say

- *What do you notice about this word? It begins with the letter sound ...*
- *What other words do you know that begin with that sound?*
- *What other words do you know that end with the same letter sounds?*
- *Can you give me a rhyming word?*
- *Have you seen those letters together before?*
- *Look at the shape of the word ...*
- *Do you remember reading that sentence on the last page? It's the same sentence here ...*
- *Read that bit again and tell me a word that fits and makes sense ...*
- *Look at the picture. What do you think this word could be?*

The place of dictionaries, wall charts, spell checks, pictures ...

Dictionaries, wall charts, spell checks, picture dictionaries and clues of any type have their place in analytic phonics for supporting reading and writing.

Summary

In political circles, analytic phonics has lost favour. However, research continues in the field of SEN, especially in relation to the needs of **dyslexic** children. (See Chapter 10 for more information about phonics and those who find learning to read more challenging than most.)

Teachers still enjoy borrowing some of the analytic techniques for exploring picture books or story books that are not intended for an ensured independent read but for developing skills of **comprehension**, for example.

So, in analytic phonics children often analyse the letters and sounds of a word once they know it; in synthetic phonics the knowledge of letters and sounds supports the child to know how to pronounce or spell a word.

In analytic phonics children learn a selection of sight-words to get started. They then move on to looking at initial sounds and when they know the letter sounds they may be encouraged to use these to help them to decode. In synthetic phonics children are encouraged to use their letter sound knowledge to read and spell very early on. Once they know **s**, **a**, **t**, **p** they can read *at*, *sat*, *pat*, *tap* and many can also begin to spell.

Synthetic phonics is current parlance and practice. Watch this space ...!

CHAPTER 3 BLENDING AND SEGMENTING

What you need to know

Once the children have begun to master the relationship between letters and sounds (**grapheme–phoneme** correspondences) they need to begin using these in words as quickly as possible, for both reading and spelling. **Blending** and **segmenting** are the processes used to achieve this.

Learning to blend and segment begins with simple oral work, then simple reading and simple spelling. The progression is as follows:

1. Check that the children can hear and say sounds and then blend them together to hear and say a word (see **sound-talk** page 24).

> Good listening and speaking skills and oral **comprehension** always underpin developing literacy skills for both reading and writing.

2. Check that the children can respond to a grapheme by saying the matching sound; so they see the letter **m** and say /m/ and in time they see the word **man** and decode it /m//a//n/ to read **man**. Eventually they no longer need to decode because their **decoding** has become implicit and automatic.

3. Check that the children can hear a sound and produce the matching grapheme for it; so they hear /b/ and know they should write the letter **b** and in time they hear or say the word **boat** and encode it /b//oa//t/ in order to write **boat**. Eventually they no longer need to encode because their encoding has become implicit and automatic.

> You need to know that blending and segmenting are two sides of the same coin. Both are focused on using letter and sound knowledge of real words to read or to spell. We blend to read and segment to spell. The goal is automaticity, **comprehension** and clarity of communication.

Reading

Blending is the process by which we decode letters (graphemes) into sounds (phonemes) in order to read. The quicker children decode, the sooner they can begin to comprehend; the more they comprehend, the more they appreciate that reading is for pleasure and for learning.

Decoding must be rapid and become automatic so that the children can begin to focus on comprehending what they are reading. Beware the child who can decode brilliantly but has no idea what he or she is reading – this is not the end goal!

Spelling

Spelling requires segmenting skills. Initially spelling is harder to grasp than reading, so children will read words before they can spell them. Note that in *Letters and Sounds* the spelling of **high-frequency words**, for example, follows a session focused on reading those same words.

Invented spelling, is the practice of spelling unfamiliar words by making an educated guess as to the correct spelling.

In **synthetic phonics** children will be taught, practise and apply segmenting skills in a systematic sequence, in their daily **phonics** lesson. They should be spelling words we know they are able to segment.

A note about ...

Talk

Reading and writing both depend upon oral language skills and comprehension. The more children talk and read the more their vocabulary grows, and the more their vocabulary grows the more words they have to draw upon for writing. If children do not read, they will not be good writers.

Sound-talk

Sound-talk is referred to in many different ways in different programmes, e.g. Robot Talk, a generic term used in *Letters and Sounds*, or Fred Talk. In sound-talk the word is spoken aloud phoneme by phoneme in order to work out the whole word.

Mnemonics

Mnemonics are tricks to help us remember things and all systematic synthetic phonics programmes will have mnemonic systems of some kind.

The chart on the following page outlines some important points about using mnemonics in synthetic phonics teaching.

Positive benefits of using mnemonics

- Simple, lively mnemonics can help children to learn phonemes and their corresponding graphemes.

- Provide representative words and pictures for each phoneme (usually in the initial position in a word) to support phoneme recognition.

- Children initially only read the first grapheme and not necessarily the whole word, since in the early stages a word like *apple* is not yet decodable.

- Provide representative words and pictures for each grapheme as well as a reference for correct letter formation not only to support the recall of sounds, but also to act as a quick check for spelling alternatives.

- The children can use mnemonic charts to remind themselves of spellings, e.g. for /igh/, so they can decide which of -**igh** or -**y** they need for the word they are trying to spell.

- An alphabet frieze is a useful resource for children and teachers to share when discussing spelling options. Such is the alphabet frieze from Oxford University Press, Oxford Reading Tree Floppy's Phonics Sounds and Letters (below), showing letters in capital and lower-case form with mnemonic pictures.

Checks

- Ensure that the children do not become over-dependent upon the pictures so they learn the associated image rather than the grapheme or phoneme, e.g. children may say '*apple*' when they see the grapheme **a** rather than the phoneme /a/ since they rely on the image that has stuck in their mind.

- Ensure that your chosen programme offers letters (and eventually words too) with and without picture cues. For example, a **flashcard** may have the letter **m** on one side and the picture of a *mountain* (or mnemonic image) on the reverse, as shown in the example below from Oxford University Press.

- Having the letter and picture on the same side is far less useful than having the letter on one side and the mnemonic image on the reverse.

- Mnemonics only work if they are used consistently across a programme so they become iconic, in the way that we all associate **a** with *apple*.

- Ensure that the children can hear or see the letter in different places in the word – clearly this is unavoidable with words such as *buzz* or *fox*, where the letters fall at the end of the word. However, can they hear the /p/ in *pan* and *ape*? And in a word like *bottle* can they hear the different sounds – the initial /b/, the middle /t/ and the final /ul/?

- Mnemonics should not only exist for the simple sounds (one letter, one sound and two letters, one sound) but for all 44 phonemes.

Blending techniques

Five steps to blending

 See a word in print, e.g. **cat.**

 Point under each letter or group of letters as you say each sound in the word from left to right: **c – – a – – t.**

 Say the sounds again faster, and then again even faster, to blend them until you can hear the whole blended word: **c-a-t**, *cat*!

 As you say the word run your finger under it: *cat*.

Tweak or modify the pronunciation of the word if you need to.

A note about ...

Dots, dashes and sound buttons

These are often used in order to help children notice the phonemes in a word. Read more about them in Chapter 2.

Sequence

Words of any length and complexity may be blended including CV, CVC, CCVC and CVCC, two-syllable words and even polysyllabic words. It's quite usual to tackle polysyllabic words by blending them syllable by syllable and then putting the syllables back together: ***chimpanzee:* ch-i-m chim, p-a-n pan, z-ee zee – chim-pan-zee – *chimpanzee*!**

Similarly, single words, captions, phrases and sentences may all be blended.

High-frequency and tricky words and tweaking

Many high-frequency words are spelled regularly and can be decoded easily. Even **tricky words** may be blended using the **phonics** children know and then tweaking them a bit (which comes with practice). For example, **of** – /o//f/ does not sound quite right so encourage the children to try /v/ to get to /o//v/ – **of**! Model this for children, but don't let them start guessing and don't let them struggle too much either – better to model how you do it and/or give them the word.

Decodable books

Once the children have a good foundation of letters and sounds they will need to practise their blending skills. Use the activity ideas below but also use specially created decodable texts at the correct phonic level to ensure that the children can read them independently with success.

The place of pictures

Pictures have their place in many texts, encourage discussion and enjoyment, and may even offer valuable information. However, for blending practice children need decodable texts and should not be encouraged to think that reading is a guessing game. Pictures should not be used to prop up poor decoding skills in independent reading situations – save them for reading for pleasure.

Rules

Children need to learn rules that can inform their blending skills. In the earliest stages they learn that **c**, **k** and **ck** are all code for /k/; this can help them to read words such as **cat**, **kick** and **kip**. They learn to say one sound for double letters such as **ff**, **ll**, **ss** and so on. As they become more proficient they learn more sophisticated rules such as how to blend **-ed** endings which may be code for /d/, /t/ or /e//d/, as in **rained**, **jumped** and **decided**.

Ten oral blending activities

1. **Give instructions** to the children in sound-talk, e.g: *It's home t-igh-m **time**! Let's go out to p-l-ay **play**!*.
2. **Use a puppet or toy**, and pretend it is shy and can only speak in sound-talk, e.g: *Pop is very shy. He says he wants to go out to play. He says he wants to j-u-m-p. What does he want to do?* Or encourage the children to ask the puppet questions in a similar manner.

A glove puppet is fun to use and easy to make.

3. **Say something wrong**, e.g:
   This is my s-o-ck, as you put on your coat.
   The children will soon correct you.

4. **Hide simple items in a sound box.**
   Say:
   In my box I have a ... d-o-g.
   When the children say ***dog***, pull out the dog to reward them. Repeat the sounds with the children and say the word.

5. **Have some small objects set out.**
   Say:
   I'm choosing the ... l-ea-f. When the children say ***leaf***, repeat the sounds and say the word together.

6. **At home time or play time**, give out cards that feature pictures of CVC words.
   Say:
   *You may go if you have the ... **t-a-p, z-i-p, b-a-t***, etc.
   Each child who has the picture must say the sounds, say the word, hand it in and go!

7. **Play the above game in reverse.**
   Have all the children standing up.
   Say:
   Sit down if you are wearing g-r-ee-n. Children wearing green sit down and you say:
   Sit down if you are wearing p-i-nk.
   Ask one or two of the children already sitting to repeat **p-i-nk** and say ***pink***. Before the children sit down, ask them to show you what they are wearing that is pink! Continue until all of the children are sitting.

8. **Play 'I Spy' using sound-talk.**
   Say:
   I spy with my little eye a ... b-a-g. Invite a child to say the sounds, say the word and find the object. If they can, it is their turn to spy something.

9. **Play 'Please may I have ...?'**
   Say to a particular child
   _____, please may I have a blue p-e-n?
   The child must get up and find a blue pen for you. You say:
   Th-a-nk y-oo. Then select another item.

10. **Play the train game.**
    Choose a child to start. The child says:
    I got on the train with a c-a-t – **cat**! *I choose* [another child] *to join the train.*
    The chosen child gets up and joins the train (a line) and says:
    I got on the train with a p-e-n – a pen! I choose ..., and so on.
    Keep playing until all the children are standing in a long train line. Some children will need help with this.

Ten blending activities

These games can be played at most phases if the words are carefully selected.

1. Use sound buttons

Teach blending of VC or CVC words, e.g. *if*, *map*. Instead of just pointing to the letters as you say the sounds – put a button, dot or blob under each letter or group of letters that represents a sound, as shown on the examples below (in the case of VC or CVC words each letter will represent one sound but, at later phases, more than one letter may represent a single sound, e.g. **br/igh/t**. In this case, **igh** would only need a single line underneath it). This is sound-talk but with a visual clue. Write up simple VC or CVC words and invite children to add the blob.

$$i \; f \qquad m \; a \; p \qquad b \; r \; \underline{igh} \; t$$

2. Use word cards

Play class 'Bingo'. Use six pictures stuck on the board as a giant Bingo card. Pick out a word card (all words to be simple VC or CVC). The child picking out the card must blend the word, read it (with help from the class if necessary) and match it to the correct picture. When all the pictures have a word attached – you shout 'Bingo'.

3. Use large letter cards

Three children are each given a large letter card and asked to stand together to make a word. The rest of the class say the sounds and read the word. Choose another trio of children to make a word if practising CVC, or more children if you are practising CCVC or CVCC words.

4. Change the word

As above but change one letter each time to make a different word. Sometimes it's possible to end with the same word you started with. This is known as Full Circle, e.g. *cat*, *cap*, *tap*, *tip*, *dip*, *pip*, *pit*, *pat*, *cat* – Full Circle! This is great for both blending and segmenting.

5. Beat the clock

Show a pre-selected list of words for children. Try to read as many words as possible in a set time. Once the timer is set, invite the children one at a time to sound-talk and then read a word. *Splash Phonics* for the interactive whiteboard (available from Rising Stars) has a series of unit reviews which would enable you to play this game very easily with its on-screen sand timer.

6. What's in the bag?

Have a bag of objects to match the words you wish to practise reading. Tubs of small objects per phoneme are commercially available from companies such as E. J. Arnold and TTS Group. Show a word, ask a child to sound it out, read it, then find the matching object in the bag.

7. Human dominoes

Hand out a large set of dominoes that feature words and (not matching) pictures. Choose a child to start. The child who has the picture to match the word on the first domino must stand up. The child who has the picture to match the next word then stands up. Continue until all the dominoes have been used.

8. **Change it**

   Write a caption, phrase or sentence that is decodable for the children. Ask the children to blend it and read it. Then remove or erase one word and write a new one. Invite the children to again blend and read the new word. Continue for as long as you can, changing just one word each time.

9. **Yes or no**

   When children can read simple sentences, prepare some silly sentences. In pairs or groups, children must read the questions and decide whether to hold up their 'Yes' or 'No' card. Ensure the children blend the sentence for the class as well as justifying their response.

   > *Can a dog hop?*
   > *Can a rat sit in a bin?*
   > *Is a bus red?*

10. **Draw it**

    Prepare some simple sentences. In pairs ask the children to respond in drawing, e.g. a pig on a log, a bus on top of a hut, etc. Invite the children with the best drawing to demonstrate the blending of the sentence for the others.

Segmenting techniques

Seven steps to segmenting

Say a word quite slowly, e.g. **map**.

Orally segment the word by identifying each sound in it – you can hold up a finger for each sound you say to help the children see the number of sounds.

> The box in which you may write each grapheme is often called a *phoneme frame* and looks like this:
>
> | m | a | p |
> |---|---|---|

Repeat as above but draw a box or a line for each sound or for each finger held up.

Repeat as above but now write a letter (or letters) for each sound on the line or in each box you have drawn.

> As children become more proficient so the need for a box or line will be reduced until it is no longer needed.

Check that the letters you have written down, when blended, say the word you are trying to write.

Correct any errors by returning to select a different grapheme.

As you do the final check, say the word and run your finger under it.

A note about ...

Sequence

Words of any length and complexity may be segmented including CV, CVC, CCVC, CVCC, two-syllable words and even polysyllabic words. It's quite usual to tackle polysyllabic words by segmenting them syllable by syllable, writing each syllable and then putting the syllables back together to write the whole word. For example, alphabet has three syllables: **al-pha-bet**. Children may write **a-l al**, **ph-a pha**, **b-e-t bet** to make the whole word **_alphabet_**. Similarly, single words, captions, phrases and sentences may all be segmented in stages.

TOP TIP

What you can say

- *Let's try to hear how many sounds are in this word.*
- *Say the word, sound it out.*
- *Show me a finger (or let's write a box/line) for each sound in the word.*
- *Let's write a letter/letters for each sound in the word.*
- *Let's check that we have written the right sounds to make this word.*

High-frequency and tricky words and tweaking

Even tricky words may be segmented using the phonics you know and then tweaking them a bit (which comes with practice). For example, children may try to write **_there_** as **_their_** or **_they're_** and only with understanding rules and becoming more confident with spelling options do they make fewer errors. Model this for children when they want to spell a tricky word and encourage them to have a go first on their own, as they can often get very close. Segmenting really helps children to focus on what is genuinely the tricky part of the word, rather than thinking that the whole word is tricky.

The place of dictionaries, wall charts and spell checks

Dictionaries, wall charts and spell checks all have their place in supporting a child to write and they provide valuable discussion opportunities. However, for segmenting practice, in the early stages especially, the children need to be presented with challenges and topics that include vocabulary they can encode. So use these other important strategies and resources elsewhere, but not in your daily phonics lesson.

Rules

Children need to learn some spelling rules that can inform their segmenting skills. In the earliest stages they quickly learn that to write a simple word such as **_game_**, they will need to make choices: **_gaim_**, **_gaym_** or **_game_**. They learn that they write two letters for some single sounds such as **ch** and **sh** and three letters for some such as **air** and **ear**. As they become more proficient they learn more sophisticated rules such as how to use prefixes, suffixes and syllables.

Ten segmenting activities

1. Oral toy-talk

As in blending, there is a host of opportunities to use a toy or puppet for developing this skill. Tell the children that the puppet only understands sound-talk and invent situations where you have to segment a word for the puppet. E.g. *What shall we give the puppet to eat? **A bun.*** The children then have to segment the word ***bun*** – **b-u-n** with you as you give it to the puppet.

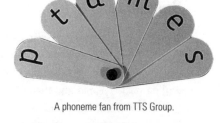

A phoneme fan from TTS Group.

2. Which item?

When the children are confident to sound-talk they can play a kind of oral segmenting 'I Spy'. They see a collection of items (pre-selected by you in a bag or on a table) and one child secretly chooses an item. He or she sound-talks it for the others. The others must blend it to reveal the correct word and item.

3. Phoneme frames

Prepare two, three, four or more box phoneme frames, depending on which stage you are at (see page 116). Use card frames, small magnetic whiteboards with magnetic letters, mini whiteboards or the interactive whiteboard. Children say a word, say it in sound-talk, establish the number of phonemes in the word, find the letters and build the word. You can model this first and then ask the children to work in pairs.

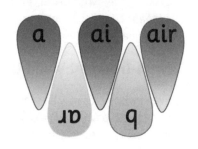

Phoneme fan parts from Free Early Years Teaching Resources, www.earlylearninghq.org.uk.

4. Phoneme fans

As above but using fans, which you can purchase or make. Fans are made with a designated set of letters, or letters can be written onto blank laminated fans, to be used by children in pairs to practise spelling.

5. Change the word

As above, but change one letter each time to make a different word. Sometimes it's possible to end with the same word you started with and this is known as Full Circle, e.g. ***clat***, ***clap***, ***clip***, ***flip***, ***flap***, ***flat***, ***clat*** – Full Circle! This is great for both blending and segmenting and can be played to include pseudo-words as in the above example.

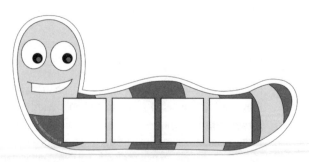

Whopper Phonic Worm from Sweet Counter.

6. **Washing line**

   Peg up selected grapheme cards on a washing line across the classroom or peg up socks which feature each chosen grapheme. You say a word and the children must get the correct graphemes from the washing line to make the word and peg it out in the right order.

7. **A quiz**

   Prepare about five questions. The answers must be words children can encode. They write the answers in pairs on paper or on mini whiteboards. You can theme these quizzes, e.g. traditional tales/nursery rhymes – *What colour hood has Riding Hood got?* (red), etc.

8. **Caption it!**

   Show the children how to use their segmenting skills to write simple captions to accompany pictures. Decide on a simple caption, e.g. *a **rat** and a **bat***, and show the children how to segment each word in order to write it.

9. **Clap it**

   Make a list of two- or three-syllable words when the children are at about *Letters and Sounds* Phase 3. Say the word ***rainbow***, clap the syllables **rain/bow**, clap the first word ***rain***, segment the sounds in it **r-ai-n**, then repeat for the second syllable. Read both syllables of the word to read ***rainbow***.

10. **Say what you know**

    Practise spelling high-frequency tricky words such as ***no***. Sound-talk the word, /n//oa/, establishing that there are two sounds. Write **n** and **oa**. Ask the children if that is right. Explain that **oa** does say /oa/ but we have to learn that we write **o** in this case. So the children have used what they know to tweak their spelling of a high-frequency tricky word.

CHAPTER 4 HIGH-FREQUENCY WORDS, TRICKY WORDS — WHAT ARE THEY AND HOW DO WE TEACH THESE?

What are high-frequency words?

High-frequency words are the words that are most common in the English language. The many high-frequency words listed in *Letters and Sounds* come from a study into books published for children to read. The first 25 make up about one-third of all printed material and the first 100 make up about half of all printed material, so they're really very useful to learn and they are listed below in order of frequency.

1. the	26. are	51. do	76. about
2. and	27. up	52. me	77. got
3. a	28. had	53. down	78. their
4. to	29. my	54. dad	79. people
5. said	30. her	55. big	80. your
6. in	31. what	56. when	81. put
7. he	32. there	57. it's	82. could
8. I	33. out	58. see	83. house
9. of	34. this	59. looked	84. old
10. it	35. have	60. very	85. too
11. was	36. went	61. look	86. by
12. you	37. be	62. don't	87. day
13. they	38. like	63. come	88. made
14. on	39. some	64. will	89. time
15. she	40. so	65. into	90. I'm
16. is	41. not	66. back	91. if
17. for	42. then	67. from	92. help
18. at	43. were	68. children	93. Mrs
19. his	44. go	69. him	94. called
20. but	45. little	70. Mr	95. here
21. that	46. as	71. get	96. off
22. with	47. no	72. just	97. asked
23. all	48. mum	73. now	98. saw
24. we	49. one	74. came	99. make
25. can	50. them	75. oh	100. an

Letters and Sounds sets out high-frequency and **tricky words** in order of difficulty and whether they are **decodable** or tricky. However, there are discrepancies, since the following are listed as decodable but are not immediately so:

a is usually pronounced as /ai/ not /a/   **as** is pronounced as /a//z/

is is pronounced as /i//z/   **of** is pronounced as /o//v/

Most words are decodable once you know the rule or know how to tweak a sound.

How to teach a high-frequency word

The children should learn to read words before they are asked to spell them. At the beginning (*Letters and Sounds* Phase 2) they practise **blending** and reading CV high-frequency words: *it*, *in*, *at* before progressing to the CVC word **and**.

a n d

It's useful to have these high-frequency words on cards with sound buttons under each letter. You may choose to begin with a CV word, but the example above is CVC:

1. **Sound-talk** the word for the children: this involves saying each sound as you point to each letter: /a//n//d/. It is sometimes referred to as 'Robot Talk'.
2. Say the word.
3. Repeat the sound-talk and get the children to say the word to you or a partner.
4. Repeat with a few more words that are either CV or CVC.
5. Show another word and ask the children to sound-talk it with you – all together. After each sound it's essential that you say the sound before they continue. Then they say the word and you should say it back to confirm that they have blended the sounds correctly. Repeat this with up to about eight more simple words.
6. Repeat step 5 above but without you confirming the sounds each time. The children try sound-talking the sounds on their own and then saying the word to a partner or together. They can try several words to really gain confidence with the process.

TOP TIP

Many teachers find it helpful to use a puppet or toy for the sound-talk and some commercial programmes provide these as part of the package. The fun is that the 'toy' can make mistakes, which the children love to spot!

There are lots of variations for this basic procedure, such as:

 Have the children blend to read a word and then match it with an object which may be in the classroom or in a 'magic box' or similar.

 Have the children blend to read a word and then match it to a picture from a selection displayed on a board or table.

Split the class in two. One-half have word cards to read whilst the others have pictures that match the words. The children holding the cards must sound-talk or read the word so that the child holding the matching picture can find his or her partner. See pages 113–119 for more game ideas.

What are tricky words?

Tricky words are common words in the English language with unusual or less obvious spellings.

In *Letters and Sounds* and most commercial schemes they are listed as high-frequency tricky words. There are also high-frequency decodable words, but the point is that they are all tricky until you have been taught the **phonics**. In reality, there are very few words that remain truly tricky – and, for those that do, you just have to apply the phonics you know, try to work it out, note which bit of the word is causing problems and then tweak until you work it out. This 'tweaking' skill is an important one to nurture. For more about tweaking, see Chapter 3.

In the past we have usually suggested that children learn these words by various methods other than phonics:

 sight memory   word shape

 beginning

letter pattern   colour.

The problem with these techniques is that they often rely on an exceptionally good memory and/or unnatural props. In the real world you just have to be able to understand the code, and phonics gives you the simplest and most reliable starting point.

You may have heard of a technique called 'Look, say, cover, write, check' (LSCWC), which was a **mnemonic** for a strategy we wanted children to try when they were learning these words. This is no longer a popular strategy since a phonics first approach will most usually help the children to crack the code to read or spell a word.

However, as children become more proficient we do start to make links with spelling, which involves understanding and knowledge of syllables, patterns such as **ing** and **ed**, prefixes and suffixes.

How to teach a tricky word

Tricky words are best met in the context of simple phrases, captions or sentences.

Some examples are given in the chart below.

Phase	Example captions, phrases and sentences	
2	a cat and a dog in a cot I can go to the top of the hill	a rat on the red mat
3	Jill had a chat with her mum. She was sad. We are on the way back now.	I can get the bus into town. You can join me.
4	I said I must help him. What did those little children like?	Come with me.
5	I looked at Mrs Smith when she called me. The people called out to us and we felt annoyed.	I asked if I could stay at home.
6	The small dog was playful with their ball. We love to visit them at the seaside but they are going away. Who said there would be bowls of soup for us at the zoo café?	

Children easily understand the notion that there are some tricky areas, but here are six tips for guiding them.

1. Read the caption or phrase, pointing to each word, then zoom in on the tricky word you want to focus on. Repeat that word.
2. Isolate the word – write it on a board of some kind and sound-talk it.
3. Sound-talk it again, add sound buttons (see Chapter 2) under each **phoneme** and blend them to read it (you have to tweak as you go, to model to the children how you have to adapt some letter sounds to make sense of the word).
4. Talk to the children about which part of the word is tricky – where the letters do not match to the sounds the children know, e.g. in *no*, the last letter does not say /o/ but /oa/.
5. Read the word again and explain that these tricky bits crop up from time to time. Keep finding opportunities to revisit the word frequently so the children are reminded of it and can begin to embed the learning.
6. Get the children to make up their own captions, phrases or sentences using tricky words.

Tips for teaching and learning high-frequency and tricky words

Don't

- avoid high-frequency or tricky words – they are common words and need to be learned
- try to sound out each **grapheme**, /t/, /h/, /e/ will not help you to blend **the**
- forget to look for bits of the word that are known – build on knowledge
- expect a child to spell a word before he or she can read it
- struggle for ages – better to tell the child the word and move on.

> **TOP TIP**
>
> It is not possible to show the phonemes for the word **one** – it's one you just have to learn!

Do

- teach the words systematically for reading and spelling
- flag up some of the basic rules for the children:

  - Many words in English end with letter **e** which we do not sound out.

  - If there is a **vowel** in the word, try blending with the short vowel sound, but if that doesn't work then try again with the long vowel phoneme. It's not /m/, /a/, /k/, so try /m/, /ai/, /k/.

  - Two of the same **consonant** letters in a word equal one sound, as in **little**, where the two **t**s represent one sound, /t/.

  - The letters **ed** can be code for /d/, /t/ or /e + d/ as in **called**, **looked** and **uploaded**.

- try to blend, and then try again if it doesn't make sense, e.g. **of** – /o/, /f/ and then try again to get – /o/, /v/.

Ensure that the children get daily practice of reading these high-frequency and tricky words in order to be able to recognise them quickly. Read words, captions, sentences to constantly reinforce knowledge and skills so that reading becomes automatic.

> **TOP TIP**
>
> It's useful to have a bank of captions ready for each phase so that you can offer practice that is quick, easy and accessible.

Memory-triggers

Memory-triggers or mnemonics are simple tricks that help us to remember things. They work best when they are personalised. In phonics they have to be used carefully to ensure that children don't over rely on them, so it's very important that the children see letters with no visual cue as well as using the mnemonics in the early stages. Most commercial schemes provide key or iconic pictures and key words across resources.

It is important that reading and spelling do not become guessing games, so always use a 'phonics first' approach.

More teaching ideas

Try some of these ideas to help the children learn tricky words using a phonics-based approach.

- An iconic image for each letter and sound can be helpful. So, for example, a teddy and the word **teddy** associated with the letter and sound /t/ may help when a child is struggling to work out a different word with the same ending, such as **happy**. You can say to the child: *You need the same /ee/ sound as the end of* **'teddy'**. Most commercial schemes have an iconic image in this way, so use them to your advantage and don't be afraid to return to them for more sophisticated teaching and learning.

- The sound /k/ needs a mnemonic for the letters **c**, **k** and **ck**. You might say to a child: *You need /k/ as in* **'duck'** *not* **'cat'**.

- Encourage the children to 'try out' their phonic knowledge to arrive at the most likely best blend or spelling – *tweak* and go for the *best bet*!

- Try to sound-talk a word by exaggerating the letter sounds, as if speaking like a robot, to model how to use phonic skills to read a word.

- Some schemes use dots and dashes to help the children with identifying the number of letters per phoneme for reading and/or spelling:

    c o me   l i tt le

- Try grouping words into families to help the children. The chart on page 40 includes the high-frequency tricky words given in *Letters and Sounds* for Phases 2–5.

By letter sound	By letter(s): same/similar letters different pronunciation and/or different letters same pronunciation	By topic	Oddities
i as /igh/ *I*	*the* *they* *their* *there*	*one, two, three, four, five, six, seven,* *eight, nine, ten*	*are* *the*
e as /ee/ *me, we, he, she, be*	*said* *again*	*people* *Mr, Mrs, Miss* *father, mother, brother, sister*	*our* *one*
o as /oo/ *to, do, into*	*her, were* *here*	*call, called* *ask, asked* *look, looked* *like liked*	
o as /oa/ *no, go, so, oh no!*	*you, your, our* *out, about*	*you, your, our* *out, about*	
y as /igh/ *my, try, cry, sky*	*come* *some*	*to* *two* *too*	
s as /z/ *is, as, was, because*	*goes* *does* *shoes*	*of* *off*	
ould as /oo//d/ *could, should, would*		*big* *little*	
all as /all/ *all, call, called*			

CHAPTER 5 WHAT TO TEACH AND IN WHAT ORDER (INCLUDING HIGH-FREQUENCY WORDS)

The content and sequence of **phonics** teaching is relatively easy to decide, now that the DfE openly supports the case for systematic **synthetic phonics**.

As part of its commitment to synthetic phonics, the DfE has:

- Commissioned and published a battery of reports and documents which outline the evidence nationally and internationally for systematic synthetic phonics.

- In association with the National Literacy Strategy, published a programme for schools to follow *Letters and Sounds*.

- Specified criteria for systematic synthetic phonic resources and training.

- Created an online list of approved resources and training that can be found on the DfE website: www.education.gov.uk/.

- Worked with Ofsted to ensure that inspectors receive phonics training to better understand what to look for in schools, and to specify that inspectors may hear the children read in order to make judgements about a school's approach to teaching early reading.

- Worked with initial teacher training agencies to ensure that establishments teach trainees how to teach reading using a systematic synthetic phonics approach.

- Introduced a national Phonics Screening Check for all children aged 6, the results for which must be reported (further details in Chapter 11).

So, although teaching synthetic phonics is not statutory, with so much on offer and at stake, a school would have to be extremely confident to be travelling in a different direction.

What do the DfE criteria for systematic phonic resources and training say about what to teach?

High-quality systematic phonic work as the prime approach to reading and spelling even when a word is not phonically regular including:

- grapheme–phoneme (letter–sound) correspondences (the alphabetic principle) in a clearly defined, incremental sequence

- the highly important skill of blending (synthesising) phonemes, in order, all through a word to read it

- the skills of segmenting words into their constituent phonemes to spell

- the fact that teaching blending and segmenting are reversible processes.

Simple to complex essential phonic knowledge and skills by age 6 years.

Major grapheme–phoneme correspondences – a defined initial group of consonants and vowels, enabling the children, early on, to read and spell many simple CVC words.

Blending phonemes in order, from left to right, 'all through the word' for reading.

Segmenting words into their constituent phonemes for spelling and knowing that this is the reverse of blending phonemes to read words.

Reading and spelling high-frequency words and tricky words that do not conform completely to grapheme–phoneme correspondence rules.

Reading texts (and spelling words) that are within the reach of their phonic knowledge and skills even though every single word in the text may not be entirely decodable by the children unaided.

(Based on the DfE criteria at www.education.gov.)

And when to begin to teach systematic synthetic phonics?

Teachers will make principled, professional judgements about when to start on a systematic programme of phonic work but it is reasonable to expect that the great majority of children will be capable of and benefit from doing so by the age of five. It is equally important for the programme to be designed so that children become fluent readers having secured word recognition skills by the end of key stage one.

(*Criteria for Assuring High-Quality Phonic Work*, DfE, 2010, available from www.education.gov.uk/)

What is definitely *not* part of systematic synthetic phonics teaching?

The following have been or are common strategies in the teaching of early reading skills. Whilst some are fun and may benefit aspects of language development, they are not part of a systematic synthetic **phonics** programme.

- Teaching one letter and its corresponding sound per week, going slowly.
- Learning letter sounds in alphabetical order, **a–z**.
- Saying letter sounds with 'uh' on the end, e.g. **suh** rather than **sss**.
- Never moving beyond single letters plus **ch**, **sh**, **th**.
- Only recognising/hearing *initial* letter sounds in words.
- Using pictures to 'read' words.
- Memorising words and texts or guessing words.
- Looking for visual patterns in words as clues to reading.
- Teaching 'blends' as in **cl-**, **br-** at the beginning of words, or **-nd**, **-ft** as units in their own right rather than as separate sounds.
- Relying on rhyme.
- Using analogy as in onset (the beginning of words, e.g. **br-**) and rime (the ending of words, e.g. **-ight**) to make *bright*, *light*, *fright*, *might*.
- Only teaching reading and not linking it immediately to spelling.

A note about Phase 1 and phonological awareness

There is some controversy about the value and place of phonological development in phonics programmes. Many purists claim that, while essential for early language development, **phonological awareness** as set out in *Letters and Sounds* Phase 1 is not part of systematic synthetic phonics. Much of it is about tuning children in to sounds in the broadest sense, so that they are well placed to 'hear' letter sounds when they begin to learn to read. It is not part of the core criteria as specified by the DfE and so is not included below. Further aspects of Phase 1 are covered in Chapter 7.

Phase 2

> Should take about 6 weeks.

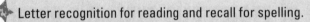

- Letter recognition for reading and recall for spelling.

- Practising oral blending for reading and segmentation for spelling.

- Reading: blending of VC words, e.g. *of*, *as*, and CVC words.

- Spelling: segmenting of VC words and CVC words.

- Introducing two-syllable words, e.g. *fusspot*.

- Tricky words: *is*, *as*, *his*, *of*, *to*, *into*, *no*, *go*, *I*, *the*.

What should the children be learning at this point?

At this phase the children should already be able to distinguish between speech sounds and many will be able to blend and segment orally (hearing **c-a-t** and knowing it is code for the word *cat*, or hearing *cat* and being able to say **c-a-t** to spell it orally).

They now learn at least 19 letters and move from mainly oral work to understanding that these sounds are represented by specific letters or graphemes. They learn that letters represent sounds and how to blend them very simply to read and spell VC and CVC words such as *if* or *cat*, or very simple two-syllable words such as *sunset*.

TOP TIP

Remember that magnetic boards and letters are a really effective hands-on resource for helping the children to manipulate the letters to practise using their reading and spelling skills. These are now commonly available in high street stores or from educational resource suppliers.

TOP TIP

It's useful to have mini-collections of objects to hand for each of the letters such as TTS Group's Sound and Spelling Tubs. Children can build vocabulary but also say the word, listen out for the target sound and identify whether it's at the beginning or end of the word.

⭐ They practise their reading and spelling of words in isolation plus in simple captions or phrases such as *cat and dog* or *a dog in a hat*, *a sad dog*, etc.

⭐ They also learn to read some high-frequency tricky words such as *the*, *to*, *no*, *go* – learning how to use the phonics they know as a first approach.

> You should aim to teach one set per week. Different schemes teach the letters in slightly different orders but the important thing is to work fairly quickly and with a consistent sequence and to ensure that the letters presented offer children an opportunity to use them to build as many words as possible, as quickly as possible.

Letter recognition and letter formation		Reading and spelling	
Letter sets	Letters	Example cumulative words or captions	High-frequency words
1	s, a, t, p	*sat, tap, pat*	*at*
2	i, n, m, d	*a sad man*	*an, dad, it, in, and*
3	g, o, c, k	*a cat in a cot* *a dog in a pit*	*got, can, not*
4	ck, e, u, r	*rats in socks* *run in mud*	*up, get, mum*
5	h, b, f, ff, l, ll, ss	*huff and puff up the hill* *get a bus to the top*	*back, off, had, big, him, but*
			Tricky words: *is, to, the, no, go, l, into, of, his, as*

> This is a CV word. But *and* is a VCC word.

> Notice that double letters **ff**, **ll** and **ss** are taught here. This is to introduce the important rule that in the **alphabetic code** two of the same letter may represent one sound. We can also teach that these double letters never begin a word in English.
>
> In set 4, **ck** is introduced separately from **c** and **k** in set 3, yet they all represent the sound /k/. Some programmes prefer to teach these together. The important point they make is that the same sound can be represented by different letters and two different letters can make one sound.

> Common words with unusual spellings – for example, you have to know that the letter **s** can sometimes be code for /z/ to be able to read the word *is*. For many children this is not a problem – they just accept this and in doing so learn one of the fundamental rules of the alphabetic code – that letters can represent more than one sound. For others it is trickier to grasp. *Letters and Sounds* does not cite *as*, *his* or *of* as 'tricky' words, but we do so throughout this book.

Phase 3

> Should take up to about 12 weeks.

 Letter recognition for reading and recall for spelling of letters: **j, v, w, x, y, z, qu**.

 Recognition of two-letter, e.g. **ch**, or three-letter, e.g. **air**, graphemes for reading and recall for spelling.

 Letter names if not introduced earlier.

 Practising reading and spelling of VC and CVC words.

 Practising reading and writing captions and simple sentences.

 More two-syllable words, e.g. **cobweb**.

 Tricky words: *he*, *she*, *we*, *me*, *be*, *was*, *my*, *you*, *they*, *her*, *all*, *are*.

What should the children be learning at this point?

 At this phase the children should know the first 19 or so letters and be able to use them with VC words to blend phonemes to read and segment words to spell – many will be able to do the same with CVC words.

 They now learn another 25 graphemes, most of which are made up of two letters, and some of three letters. This gives them access to reading and spelling about 42 phonemes – a critical step in cracking the code. At this stage they learn just one example of a sound to match the grapheme, e.g. they learn **ow** for *cow* but not yet for *show*, which follows in a later phase.

 They practise their reading and spelling of words in isolation plus in simple captions or phrases.

 They also learn to read some more high-frequency tricky words such as *he, she, we, me, be, was, my, you, they, her, all, are* and some of the tricky words taught in Phase 2 (since reading is easier than spelling).

TOP TIP

Teach the letter names at this phase if children haven't been introduced to them yet.

Sing alphabet songs because they are fun and they may help with letter names, but remember that children need to practise recognising double letters as well as **digraphs** (two different letters that make one sound, e.g. **ck** for /k/ as in *sack*) or trigraphs (three different letters that make one sound, e.g. **air** for /air/ as in *fair*) as well.

Letter recognition and letter formation		Reading and spelling	
Letter sets	Letters	Example cumulative words or captions	High-frequency words and tricky words
6	**j, v, w** **x**: has two sounds /k//s/	*jam in the van* *a wigwam in a box*	*we, was*
7	**y, z, zz** **qu**: has two sounds /k//w/	*Can you buzz? Yes I can. Quick! Get up on the box.*	*you*
	ch, sh, th, th, ng, nk	*chip, shop, thin, that, sing, pink*	*she, they* (revisit *the*)
	ai, ee, igh, oa, oo, oo	*rain, feet, high, boat, boot, book*	
	ar, or, ur, er	*car, arm, farm* *for, farm* *fur, turn* *dinner*	*are, her*
	ow, oi	*cow, coin*	
	ear, air, ure	*hear, hair, sure*	
			Tricky words: *he, me, be, my, all*

If the final letter sets take about a week each, then that leaves 9 weeks to teach two graphemes per week in this phase.

Remember **th** has two sounds to teach – **th** in ***thin*** (soft or unvoiced) and **th** in ***that*** (voiced).

nk is sometimes taught separately from **ng**. It has the same sound but with a **k** at the end. You may see it written as /ngk/.

There will be north/south differences in pronunciation of some words like this. Teach as you speak and explain any anomalies.

This is the first time children meet the important idea of three letters for one sound.

The children already know the letter **e** is code for /e/ and they are learning in this phase that **ee** is code for /ee/. Take the opportunity to teach them that the letter **e** in these high-frequency words can also be code for /ee/, so we say ***he***, ***me***, ***be***, ***we***, ***she***.

Phase 4

Should take 4–6 weeks.

- Grapheme recognition for reading, and recall for spelling of all single, two- and three-letter graphemes taught so far.

- Teaching blending for reading of words featuring adjacent consonants, e.g. CCVC and CVCC.

- Teaching segmenting for spelling of words featuring adjacent consonants, e.g. CCVC and CVCC.

- Practising reading and writing sentences.

- Practising reading and spelling two-syllable words, e.g. *sandwich*, *starlight*.

- Tricky words: *said, so, have, like, some, come, were, there, little, one, do, when, out, what*.

What should the children be learning at this point?

- At this phase the children should know the code for the 42 phonemes and be able to blend and segment CVC words using these. They will know about two-syllable words and be able to read and spell some tricky words. They will also know the letter names.

- Here they really practise using their grapheme recognition in words that feature adjacent consonants either using:

  - Phase 2 letter sets and simple vowels and/or

  - Phase 3 letter sets and the new two- or three-letter graphemes.

- They practise their reading and spelling of words with adjacent consonants in phrases or sentences.

- They learn that there may be three adjacent consonants in some words, e.g. CCCVC such as in *strip* or CCVCC as in *twist*.

- They also learn to read some more high-frequency tricky words such as *said, so, have, like, some, come, were, there, little, one, do, when, out, what*.

- They learn to spell some of the tricky words taught in Phase 3.

- They move from just reading and spelling two-syllable words to reading and spelling polysyllabic words such as *chimpanzee* or *thunderstorms*.

TOP TIP

In the past it has been common to refer to adjacent consonants as 'blends' and we have offered the children word beginning choices such as **cl**, **br**, **st** and word-endings such as **lt**, **mp**, **and**. However, in synthetic phonics we stress the importance of recognising these as separate phonemes and the importance of blending right through a word rather than jumping to stick letter strings on the beginning or the end as a fixed unit. Make sure the children can identify each sound in a word and blend right through to read it.

> This is the first time children meet the important idea of adjacent consonants.

Adjacent consonant			
Using ...	Example words CVCC	Example words CCVC, CCV	Example words CCVCC, CCCVC, CCCVCC
Phase 2 simple letter sets	b-a-n-d t-e-n-t m-i-l-k s-o-f-t h-u-n-t	t-r-a-p s-n-a-ck s-t-e-p s-n-i-ff d-r-o-p p-l-u-m	s-t-a-n-d b-l-e-n-d g-l-i-n-t f-r-o-s-t p-l-u-m-p
Phase 3 graphemes: **ch, sh, th, th, ng, nk**	ch-i-m-p b-e-n-ch sh-i-f-t th-a-nk t-e-n-th	Sh-r-e-k sh-r-i-nk th-r-u-sh s-t-i-ng s-t-i-nk	th-r-i-f-t c-r-u-n-ch s-c-r-u-n-ch
ai, ee, igh, oa, oo, oo	p-ai-n-t r-oa-s-t b-oo-s-t	t-r-ai-l s-t-ee-p b-r-igh-t s-t-oa-t s-p-oo-n	s-p-r-ai-n s-t-r-ee-t
ar, or, ur, er	b-ur-s-t f-ar-m-er	s-t-ar-t s-t-ar s-p-or-t	f-l-oa-t-er
ow, oi	p-ow-d-er j-oi-n-t	g-r-ow-l s-p-oi-l	g-r-ow-l-er s-p-oi-l-er
ear, air, ure	h-ear f-air s-ure	s-t-air f-l-air	
Polysyllabic words	*windmill* *sandwich*	*starlight* *treetop*	*driftwood*
Tricky words	*said, so, have, like, some, come, were, there, little, one, do, when, out, what*		

> These are one letter, one sound graphemes except for double letters **ff, ll, ss** and **ck**.

> **er** at the end of words represents a sound close to /u/ and is known as *schwa*. *Schwa* can be represented by other letters too.

Phase 5

 Reading: new graphemes, alternative pronunciations, two- to three-syllable words and more **high-frequency words**.

 Spelling: a new phoneme /zh/ as in ***treasure, beige*** and alternative spellings for each phoneme.

Tricky words: ***oh, their, people, Mr, Mrs, looked, called, asked, could***.

What should the children be learning at this point?

 At this phase the children should already be able to read and spell words that feature adjacent consonants, such as ***blend***. They will probably also be able to read some simple polysyllabic words.

 So now we need to expand on this knowledge and give them lots of practice. They'll learn new grapheme combinations, such as **ph**, and new pronunciations for known graphemes, such as **ch** in ***chin***, ***school*** and ***chef***. They will need to get faster at recognising graphemes of more than one letter and at blending them to read – they need lots of 'speed-reading'.

 In spelling, the children also need practice at choosing the right letters or letter groups to represent the sound. So they have to make choices and build up a word-specific bank of spelling knowledge.

 They also learn to read some more high-frequency tricky words such as ***oh, their, people, Mr, Mrs, looked, called, asked, could***.

 They learn to spell some of the tricky words taught in Phase 4: ***said, have, like, so, do, some, come, were, there, little, one, when, out, what***.

Practise and extend the reading and spelling of high-frequency words polysyllabic words.

I want to write the word ***photo*** so I need to think whether it begins with **f** or **ph** … or something else … and is the **o** written with just an **o** or could it be **oe** or **ow**. At least the **t** is easy!

These are all two letters but one sound.

	Reading			Spelling
New graphemes	**New pronunciations of some known graphemes**	**High-frequency words**		**Alternative spellings for each phoneme**
ay in *say* **ou** in *out* **ie** in *pie* **ea** in *eat* **oy** in *toy* **ue** in *glue* **aw** in *paw* **ir** in *girl* **ew** in *new* **oe** in *toe* **au** in *haul*	**ow**, *snow* **ie**, *field* **ea** in *head* **er** in *her* **ou** in *you, would, mould*	Decodable day about, house saw your		**k, ck, qu, x, ch** for /c/ **tch** for /ch/ **g, dge** for /j/ **n(k)** for /ng/ **wr** for /r/ **c, sc** for /s/ **ch, t(ion), ss(ion, ure), s(ion, ure) c(ion, ious, ial)** for /sh/ **ve** for /v/ **a** for /a/ (in the south) **aw, au, al, our** for /or/ **ir, er, ear** for /ur/ **ou** for /ow/ **oy** for /oi/ **ere, eer** for /ear/ **are, ear** for /air/ **our** for /ure/ **our, e, u** etc. for /er/
wh in *which* **ph** in *photo*	**ch** in *school, chef*			**ph** for /f/ **wh** for /w/ **mb** for /m/ **kn, gn** for /n/
a-e in *take* **e-e** in *Pete* **i-e** in *like* **o-e** in *note* **u-e** in *June* **(y)u-e** in *cube*	**e** in *me* **i** in *mind* **o** in *told* and *no* **u** in *put* **a** in *hat, last, was*	*made, came, make* *here* *I'm, time* *don't , old* *put*		**ea** for **e** in *head* **y** for **i** in *funny* **ey** for **i** in *monkey* **(w)a** for **o** in *was* **o** for **u** in *some* **ay, a-e, eigh, ey, ei** may = /ai/ **ea, e-e, ie, y, ey, eo** may = /ee/ **y, ie, i-e** may = /igh/ **ow, oe, o-e, o** may = /o/ **u, oul, o** may = /oo/ **ew, ue,ui, ou** may = /oo/
	c in *cell* **g** in *gem* **y** in *my, gym, funny*	*very, by*		
		Tricky words *oh, their, people, Mr/Mrs, looked, called, asked, would, could, should*		

*They should now know enough phonics to be able to work these out by **decoding** and blending. They're learning **ay** and **ou** at this phase as well as **aw** and **our** for /or/.*

*These are known as split **digraphs**.*

*You may say the **a** in **hat** and **last** in the same way depending on your region. You may pronounce **put** with a short or long /oo/ depending on your region.*

Common words with unusual spellings – look to use the phonics you know and tweak until the word makes sense.

Note that we also teach a final phoneme here, /zh/ as in treasure and beige. See Letters and Sounds for example words if you aren't sure (available at www. education.gov.uk/publications/).

Phase 6

On-going throughout Year 2.

 Building reading skills to work towards automaticity, especially on-going practice with recognition of graphemes with two or more letters.

 Developing spelling strategies to ensure that the children are equipped to make informed choices:

- teaching the past tense
- adding suffixes
- spelling long words
- finding and learning tricky bits in words.
- spelling guidelines and rules

 Practising the reading and writing of words, sentences and books of all kinds for learning and pleasure.

 Developing independence as a reader and writer with greater pace, stamina, accuracy and fluency.

What should the children be learning at this point?

 At this phase the children will generally be able to read and spell many hundreds of words.

 They will be reading many words automatically and only decoding those, sound by sound, that they are unsure about. Sometimes decoding will be quite quick and silent, almost used as a quick check, whilst other times children may need to revert to sounding out aloud. But all these strategies are at their finger tips and phonics is moving into the realms of comprehension, punctuation and grammar.

 They will also be learning about specific spelling rules which they can then apply when spelling longer and more difficult words. Their phonics for spelling becomes more sophisticated as they have to make spelling choices when a phoneme can be spelled in more than one way.

 They also learn to read and spell further high-frequency tricky words such as *said*, *so*, *have*, *like*, *some*, *come*, *were*, *there*, *little*, *one*, *do*, *when*, *out*, *what*.

They learn to spell some of the tricky words taught in Phase 5: *water, where, who, again, thought, through, work, mouse, many, laughed, because, different, any, eye, friends, once, please*.

> Readers must understand what they are reading. Phase 6 builds on comprehension strategies to encourage independence and enjoyment.

Reading	Spelling
Use what the children already know about a subject or a context.	Teach regular and irregular past tense.
Work on extending vocabulary by exploring and learning new words and their meanings.	Teach suffixes: **ing**, **ed**, **er**, **est**, **ful**, **ly** and **y**.
Answering but also asking questions about a book will often help to unpick its meaning.	Teach plurals
Enjoy pictures or encourage the children to make up their own pictures in their head to think about what a sentence or story might mean. Learn how to summarise what they have read.	Teach how to spell long words: • Find words in words. • Clap syllables, identify phonemes in each syllable, write the letters for each phoneme, collate them to read the word. • Identify the base words, e.g. *baking – bake + ing*. • Use analogy; understanding of similar words, e.g. knowing *the, there, their, these, them* are all similar. • Devise a mnemonic, e.g. *necessary* – one collar [c] but two sleeves [ss] or the classic **mnemonic** for *because* – Big Elephants Can Always Understand Small Elephants. • Revert to the technique of 'Look, say, cover, write, check'.
	Teach self-help strategies: • Find another word that you can write. • Leave a gap and return to it later. • Use phonics to say the word, segment the sounds and have a go. • Try splitting a word into syllables. • Think of other words that sound the same. • Use a spelling log, posters, word banks, displays around the classroom.
	• Introduce spell-checkers and dictionaries.

> Children will be reading books of all types by now and will learn that they need different strategies for different types of book: non-fiction, poetry, stories. Now they can read, we should work hard to ensure that they choose to do so independently and continue to develop a love of reading.

CHAPTER 6 TIMING AND MODEL LESSONS

Introduction

We've already covered the fundamental principle of timing in Chapter 5, so we've established that **synthetic phonics** must be presented systematically. This means presenting the material:

- in a consistent sequence
- using consistent techniques
- using consistent terminology
- using a mix of teaching scenarios, e.g. whole class, group, paired, one-to-one and independent
- daily, actively and at pace
- and, last but not least, with a sense of fun, positivity and excitement.

Children are expected to have the **alphabetic code** cracked by the age of 6 years so that they can get on to the real business of using their **phonics** to read to learn. It's a bit like taking a series of driving lessons in which the aim is to pass the test and get on with driving, travelling and exploring; so it is with phonics for reading.

What makes a good phonics lesson?

The same principles apply to phonics as to any other teaching, so the same standard lesson outline should be a good model.

1. Review previous learning
2. Introduce the new learning focus
3. Teach the new focus
4. Practise the new focus
5. Apply the new focus
6. Keep applying the new focus
7. Assess learning

A routine is important for young children and they will quickly adapt and respond to it – in fact they will begin to anticipate it. Commercially approved systematic synthetic phonic programmes will support you with ideas and resources to use throughout the stages of a lesson or series of lessons, whilst some educational suppliers provide stand-alone hands-on resources (such as magnetic letters or mini whiteboards) which can also be extremely useful.

How long should a good phonics lesson be?

Different programmes recommend different approaches to lesson timing, but it is generally agreed that there should be a daily phonics lesson. So what does this mean for a busy classroom?

In Reception children need:

 20–30 minutes per day, to include a whole class teaching session followed by group work.

The mix of whole class teaching versus group work will vary across terms so that by Term 3 the children may be working:

 for up to 40 minutes, with about 15 minutes teaching followed by 20 minutes of group work.

Some programmes suggest that a focus is split across two distinct sessions with whole class teaching of about 30 minutes on one day followed by a longer period of group work later in the day, or even the next day.

In Year 1 the daily lesson will likely increase to 60 minutes consisting of:

 20–30 minutes revisiting known letter sounds and teaching the lesson focus

 10 minutes blending and segmenting with the new letter sound

 20 minutes for group work – oral building of a sentence, reading decodable books and practising reading and writing activities.

Lesson variation

The following chart shows how a lesson may vary according to the phase of learning (based on information provided in *Letters and Sounds*).

Lesson	Phase 2	Phase 3	Phase 4	Phase 5	Phase 6
Review	Check on any previously taught letters and sounds. Check simple oral blending and segmenting.	Check on any previously taught letters and sounds.	Check on previously taught **graphemes**.	Check previously taught graphemes and blending and segmenting words with adjacent **consonants**.	Check previously taught graphemes.
	Check **tricky words**.	Check tricky words.	Check tricky words.	Check tricky words.	Check tricky words.
Teach	A new letter and letter sound. Blending and segmenting with letters and letter sounds.	New graphemes.	Blending and segmenting of adjacent consonants.	New graphemes. New pronunciations of known graphemes. New spellings of known graphemes.	**Decoding** and reading strategies. Spelling strategies.
	One or two tricky words.	One or two tricky words.	More tricky words.	Tricky words.	
Practise	Reading and spelling simple CVC words using the new letter sound.	Blending and reading words with new graphemes.	Blending and reading words with adjacent consonants.	Blending and reading words with new graphemes.	Speed reading, automatic reading, decoding silently, decoding aloud.
		Segmenting and spelling words with new graphemes.	Segmenting and spelling words with adjacent consonants.	Segmenting and spelling words with new graphemes.	Segmenting and spelling but using spelling rules too.
Apply	Demonstrate use of new focus letter sound and tricky words in speaking, listening, reading and/or writing.	Demonstrate use of new graphemes and tricky words in speaking, listening, reading and/or writing.	Demonstrate use of words containing adjacent consonants and tricky words in speaking, listening, reading and writing.	Demonstrate use of new graphemes and tricky words in speaking, listening, reading and/or writing.	Demonstrate use of phonic reading and spelling skills in general reading and writing.
	E.g. read a word, write a word, understand a **sound-talk** word.	E.g. read or write a caption or simple sentence.	E.g. write and read sentences.	E.g. read or write sentences.	E.g. read and write across the curriculum for different purposes.

What happens in each part of the daily phonics lesson?

Different programmes may vary in the detail of the lesson plans they suggest, but generally a good lesson will look something like as follows.

1. Review previous learning

- Make sure the children have a chance to begin with practising previously learned skills. This readies then both mentally and physically for new learning.

- If you are using a program on your interactive whiteboard there should be a section which allows you to easily revisit or check out previous teaching. Make it a game and celebrate what the children already know! At the same time note any areas that appear to be less secure for re-teaching or further practice in your planning schedule.

- Make sure you are checking that the children can hear, say, read and spell when appropriate to the phase they are working within.

2. Introduce the new learning focus

- Share with the children what it is they are going to be doing and what they will learn.

- Be explicit and say something like: *Today we are going to learn a new sound. Let's look at it* (show them the letter and say the sound). Tell them what sort of sound it is (it may be a long sound, a short sound, or it may need some special technique to say it effectively, such as /th/, which needs the tongue between the teeth).

- Ask if anyone's name begins with/ends with or features this sound.

3. Teach the new focus

- At different phases of the phonics teaching sequence this will mean different things (see next bullet point). Teaching is usually whole class, uses plenty of visual aids and demands excellent modelling for the children to copy.

- Use software from a phonics program and display it on the interactive whiteboard, use a flip chart or magnetic board to show the children examples of the teaching focus, use magnetic letters, teaching letter sound cards, word cards, phoneme frames – anything to make it fun and lively, speedy and interactive.

4. Practise the new focus

 At different phases of the phonics sequence this will mean different things (see below). Practice opportunities can be whole class or a small group led by the teacher or teaching assistant following focused and specific teaching.

 Some commercial software programs have built-in practice screens for teachers to use with the children, whilst others offer notes to give ideas about how to allow the children to practise.

- inviting the children to the board to help you point to each phoneme as you blend a word

- sky-writing or air-writing a newly taught letter

- handing out large phoneme cards to different children who then physically stand next to each other to make a word, and move themselves around in order to change the word

- enjoying lots of actions that may match a **mnemonic** action, phrase or picture for a new letter sound

- rolling a die or even throwing a bean bag to practise saying a focus sound or word.

Practice may also include the use of small write-on/wipe-off whiteboards (electronic or not), or magnetic letter boards, like the one below from Learning Resources (www. learningResources.co.uk), so the children can write and share as they practise blending and segmenting.

 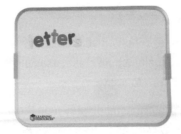 

Bean bags, magnetic letter board and dice all from Learning Resources.

5. Apply the new focus

* The children will need time to apply their new skills in different situations: small groups, pairs and independently.

* There are rafts of materials ranging from pencil and paper to software to hands-on games and equipment to make this a fun part of the lesson. The trick is to ensure that whatever you offer the children supports them to practise the specific skill taught. Ensure that they are applying their skills wherever possible for both reading and spelling, and always keep an eye on correct letter formation.

* Again, many of the resources described in point 3 above will be useful for this part of the lesson.

* All core synthetic phonic programmes will include collections of decodable books for children to read. These are books that are specifically designed to feature only the letters and sounds children know and are able to blend for reading. They serve a very specific and important purpose in providing a positive reading experience.

6. Keep applying the new focus

* Even when you are not focused on your daily phonics lesson, never miss an opportunity to consolidate new and past learning.

* Say things like: *We have five minutes before lunch time … I wonder who can read this word with me*; *Spell 'lunch'*; *Stand up if you are wearing r-e-d, b-r-ow-n*, etc.

7. Assess learning

* It is important to continually monitor a child's progress to ensure that he or she is keeping pace. Working with children in small groups or pairs, or even individually for application practice, is an ideal way to check informally whether a child has fully grasped the new teaching.

For further information on checks, monitoring and assessment, see Chapter 11.

CHAPTER 7 PHONICS, LISTENING AND SPEAKING

Introduction

The focused development of speaking and listening skills is the backbone of all early language development, and is a prime area within the Early Years Foundation Stage (EYFS). However, it is in *Letters and Sounds* Phase 1 and in the National Curriculum that we see the importance of these skills in relation to the specific development of early phonic reading skills.

Developing aural (listening) and oral (talking) skills will underpin successful routes to reading, writing and language **comprehension**.

Early Years Foundation Stage 2012

Communication and language is one of three prime areas of the EYFS:

 Listening and attention: children listen attentively in a range of situations. They listen to stories, accurately anticipating key events and respond to what they hear with relevant comments, questions or actions. They give their attention to what others say and respond appropriately, while engaged in another activity.

 Understanding: children follow instructions involving several ideas or actions. They answer 'how' and 'why' questions about their experiences and in response to stories or events.

 Speaking: children express themselves effectively, showing the awareness of listeners' needs. They use past, present and future forms accurately when talking about events that have happened or are to happen in the future. They develop their own narratives and explanations by connecting ideas or events.

(DfE, Statutory Framework for the Early Years Foundation Stage 2012)

So, the skills of speaking and listening are referenced in the prime area of communication and language, but it is in the specific area of literacy where we see focused references to phonic knowledge and skills for reading and writing.

 Reading: children read and understand simple sentences. They use phonic knowledge to **decode** regular words and read them aloud accurately. They also read some common irregular words. They demonstrate understanding when talking with others about what they have read.

 Writing: children use their phonic knowledge to write words in ways which match their spoken sounds. They also write some irregular common words and simple sentences. Some words are spelled correctly and others are phonetically plausible.

(DfE, Statutory Framework for the Early Years Foundation Stage 2012)

In the National Curriculum we continue to see the importance of these phonic skills referenced, although never formally tested apart from in the Year 1 Phonics Screening check for 6-year-olds.

DfE *Letters and Sounds*

Letters and Sounds Phase 1 references seven aspects related to the general development of listening and talk, as well as some specific aspects of **phonological awareness** and oral **blending** and **segmenting**. There is no question that these are important building blocks for early language development, but there is controversy about whether such activities systematically help the children with phonic skills and with cracking the **alphabetic code**.

The chart below shows the relationship between the different aspects, strands and the skills developed in *Letters and Sounds* Phase I.

Aspect	Strands	Skills developed
1. General sound discrimination – environmental	1. Tuning in to sounds 2. Listening and remembering sounds 3. Talking about sounds	1. Listening 2. Developing vocabulary 3. Speaking confidently 4. Visually and aurally discriminating letter sounds 5. Saying the sounds they hear in a word, in order and from beginning to end. 6. Using **sound-talk** to segment a word into its letter sounds.
2. General sound discrimination – instrumental		
3. General sound discrimination – body percussion		
4. Rhythm and rhyme		
5. Alliteration		
6. Voice sounds		
7. Oral blending and segmenting		

The following chart provides sample activity ideas for each of the seven aspects of *Letters and Sounds* Phase 1 to show how the three strands and six skills may be incorporated into provision.

Aspect/strand activity types	Tuning in to sounds: activity idea	Listening and remembering sounds: activity idea	Talking about sounds: activity idea
1. General sound discrimination – environmental	Go on a listening walk and talk about the different sounds you can hear.	Enjoy sound stories (make your own or buy pre-recorded) and then recall the sequence of the sounds heard.	Add sound effects to a story or song.
2. General sound discrimination – instrumental	Use instruments in pairs to play 'follow my leader' with a focus on volume – where one child plays and then the other copies.	Use instruments for children to play 'follow my leader' – where each child must make the same sound (pattern) as the leader.	Make up animal noises from different instruments and encourage discussion and play.
3. General sound discrimination – body percussion	Enjoy action songs.	Circle time – model a clapping pattern and pass it on around the circle.	March, stamp, jump or tiptoe to a beat.
4. Rhythm and rhyme	Sing songs and rhymes, play rhyming Bingo.	Play rhyming pairs.	Get silly with rhyming names and words.
5. Alliteration	Play 'I Spy' (using letter sound, not name).	Gran went to market and she bought (bananas, boxes, birthday cards, bins, etc.) – play in circle time.	Make silly alliterative sentences using the names of the children in the class, e.g. *Sal went swimming and surfing on Saturday.*
6. Voice sounds	Play with voice sounds, e.g. make your voice go on a seesaw – high, low, high, low – with the syllables.	Make an audio collection of voices for the class – whose voice is it?	Talk about what sort of sounds you can make – **b**, **d**, **g** are guttural and short, **m**, **s**, **z** are long sounds and **ng** is nasal and in the throat.
7. Oral blending and segmenting	Puppet talk is a popular way to engage children. The puppet blends and segments (often incorrectly) so the children in class can correct.	Repeat sound-talk accurately.	Talk about the number of sounds in a word as you play games with sound-talk.

A note about pronunciation ...

Modelling speaking and listening, interactions and talk

It is crucial to a young child's language development (including speaking, listening and **phonics**) that you:

Listen to encourage a young child to talk.

Listen to model what it is to be a good listener.

Speak using good models of spoken English (including clear pronunciation, correct grammar, wide vocabulary and in a sustained way with appropriate pace and intonation if in discussion).

In phonics, ensure that you say each letter sound or **phoneme** as purely as possible, e.g. say **ssss** not **suh**, **mmmm** not **muh**.

What is ...?

Accent: a way of pronouncing words that occurs among the people in a particular region or country, e.g. the difference between pronouncing **bath**: /b//a//th/ as opposed to /b//ar//th/.

Aural: of the ear, so most closely related to listening.

Dialect: a form of language that is spoken in a particular area and that uses some of its own words, grammar and pronunciations, e.g. **bab** as a word for **baby** in the Midlands.

Intonation: the 'song' we create whilst articulating letter sounds, words or sentences which often adds meaning to our articulation, e.g. telling the listener we are asking a question by raising the intonation at the end of the sentence.

Oral: of the mouth, so most closely related to speaking.

Oral blending and segmenting: saying each sound in a word out loud in order to then blend the sounds to be able 'hear' what the word is, e.g. *Get your c-oa-t.*

Pace: the speed with which we articulate letter sounds, words or sentences.

Phonological awareness: being alert to sounds within words, e.g. being able to say phonemes in words, produce a rhyme, count or clap syllables.

Pronunciation: the way we articulate letter sounds or words using mouth movements.

Stress: to pronounce a letter sound, syllable or word in a louder or more forceful way than other letter sounds, syllables or words in an articulation.

For further definitions and terms see the Glossary on page 120.

TOP TIP

If you need help with knowing how to say the sounds correctly there are many free online sites you can access including:

www.oxfordowl.co.uk

www.phonememachine.com/

www.phonicsinternational.com

www.bbc.co.uk/worldservice/ learning english/grammar/pron/ sounds/

THRASS®
TEACHING HANDWRITING READING AND SPELLING SKILLS

Phoneme Machine 6.1 is FREE and has a Cued Speech option!

Peculiarities of English pronunciation

Below are the first few stanzas and the last one of a poem written by Gerard Nolst Trenité (1870–1946), the whole poem can be found on the internet. If you can pronounce correctly every word in the poem you speak English better than most.

The Chaos

Dearest *creature* in *creation*
Studying English *pronunciation*,
  I will teach you in my *verse*
  Sounds like *corpse, corps, horse* and *worse*.

I will keep you, *Susy, busy*,
Make your *head* with *heat* grow dizzy;
  Tear in eye, your dress you'll *tear*;
  Queer, fair *seer, hear* my *prayer*.

Pray, console your loving *poet*,
Make my coat look *new*, dear, *sew it*!
  Just compare *heart, hear* and *heard*,
  Dies and *diet, lord* and *word*.

Sword and *sward, retain* and *Britain*
(Mind the latter how it's *written*).
  Made has not the sound of *bade*,
  Say-said, pay-paid, laid but *plaid*.

Have you ever yet *endeavoured*
To pronounce *revered* and *severed*,
  Demon, lemon, ghoul, foul, soul,
  Peter, petrol and *patrol*?

Billet does not end like *ballet*;
Bouquet, wallet, mallet, chalet.
  Blood and *flood* are not like *food*,
  Nor is *mould* like *should* and *would*.

Now I surely will not *plague* you
With such words as *vague* and *ague*,
  But be careful how you *speak*,
  Say: *gush, bush, steak, streak, break, bleak*,

Previous, precious, fuchsia, via
Recipe, pipe, studding-sail, choir;
  Woven, oven, how and low,
  Script, receipt, shoe, poem, toe.

Say, expecting fraud and *trickery:*
Daughter, laughter and Terpsichore,
  Branch, ranch, measles, topsails, aisles,
  Missiles, similes, reviles.

Wholly, holly, signal, signing,
Same, examining, but *mining,*
  Scholar, vicar, and *cigar,*
  Solar, mica, war and *far.*

From "desire": *desirable-admirable* from "admire",
Lumber, plumber, bier, but *brier,*
  Topsham, brougham, renown, but *known,*
  Knowledge, done, lone, gone, none, tone,

One, anemone, Balmoral,
Kitchen, lichen, laundry, laurel.
  Gertrude, German, wind and *wind,*
  Beau, kind, kindred, queue, mankind,

Don't you think so, reader, *rather,*
Saying *lather, bather, father?*
  Finally, which rhymes with *enough,*
  Though, through, bough, cough, hough, sough,
  tough??

[…]

Hiccough has the sound of *sup* …
My advice is: GIVE IT UP!

by Gerard Nolst Trenité

CHAPTER 8 PHONICS FOR READING – DECODING AND COMPREHENSION

What underpins phonics for reading?

Academics, teachers and the government now recognise 'The simple view of reading' model, as recommended in the *Independent Review of the Teaching of Early Reading* (2006; also known as The Rose Report). This 'model of reading' (which can also be applied to writing and necessarily impacts on speaking and listening, and which also explains **comprehension** skills), underpins most of what we need to understand about reading. The model explains a complex process in a simple way. For this reason you will find it referenced throughout this book. The simple view of reading model, from The Rose Report (page 40), is shown below.

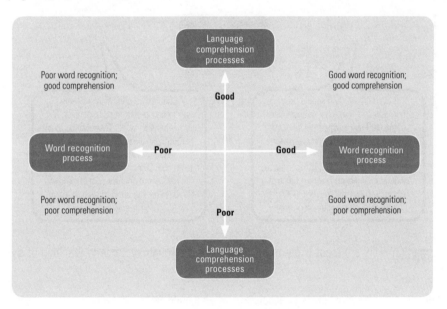

What does this mean in terms of decoding and comprehension skills?

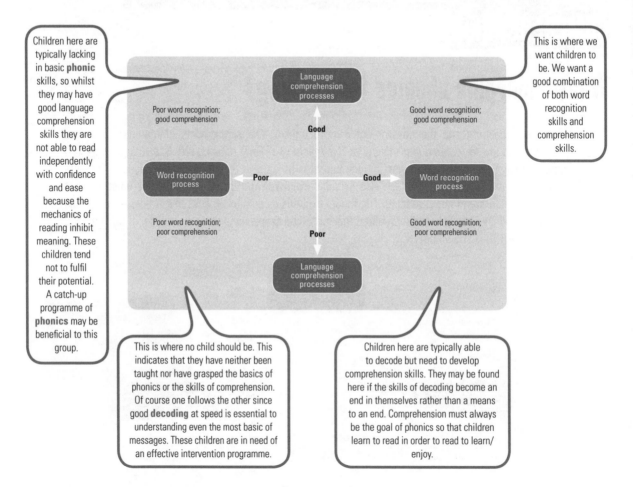

Children here are typically lacking in basic **phonic** skills, so whilst they may have good language comprehension skills they are not able to read independently with confidence and ease because the mechanics of reading inhibit meaning. These children tend not to fulfil their potential. A catch-up programme of **phonics** may be beneficial to this group.

This is where we want children to be. We want a good combination of both word recognition skills and comprehension skills.

This is where no child should be. This indicates that they have neither been taught nor have grasped the basics of phonics or the skills of comprehension. Of course one follows the other since good **decoding** at speed is essential to understanding even the most basic of messages. These children are in need of an effective intervention programme.

Children here are typically able to decode but need to develop comprehension skills. They may be found here if the skills of decoding become an end in themselves rather than a means to an end. Comprehension must always be the goal of phonics so that children learn to read in order to read to learn/enjoy.

Word recognition skills are most likely to have developed through systematic teaching of **synthetic phonics**.

Comprehension skills are most likely to accelerate when a child can read well.

What is decoding?

> *Decoding is the ability to apply your knowledge of letter–sound relationships, including knowledge of letter patterns, to correctly pronounce written words. Understanding these relationships gives children the ability to recognize familiar words quickly and to figure out words they haven't seen before.*
>
> (www.readingrockets.org/helping/target/phonics/)

The above is just one definition of decoding and much of what you need to know about decoding skills for reading has already been outlined in Chapter 3 **Blending** and **Segmenting**.

What is comprehension?

Reading comprehension is composed of two equally important components:

 Decoding – the skills of translating text into speech.

 Language comprehension – the skill of understanding spoken language.

There is often concern about whether a phonics approach to reading encourages reading for meaning and a love of reading, or simply teaches a decoding method. Here we also explore the link between decoding and comprehension in the context of the reading journey.

Language comprehension is a life-long development, whereas learning to read takes about two years. The children who have benefitted from a family situation in which talk is a frequent and common part of daily life and who talk well with a growing range of vocabulary, have the best possible chance to develop good language comprehension. And when children begin to read well independently, so their comprehension will take off. They need to complete their 'learning to read' phase so that they can get onto the real business of 'reading to learn'.

Phonics for reading in the Early Years Foundation Stage 2012

The Statutory Framework for the Early Years Foundation Stage (EYFS) specifies that any early years programme must make provision for literacy development.

> *Literacy development involves* encouraging children to link sounds and letters and to begin to read and write. *Children must be given access to a wide range of reading materials (books, poems, and other written materials) to ignite their interest.*
>
> (Statutory Framework for the Early Years Foundation Stage, page 5, emphasis added)

More specifically, within reading:

> *Children read and understand simple sentences. They use* phonic knowledge to decode regular words and read them aloud accurately. *They also read some common irregular words. They demonstrate understanding when talking with others about what they have read.*
>
> (*Statutory Framework for the Early Years Foundation Stage*, page 8, emphasis added)

So 3- to 5-year-olds are expected to tackle the most basic principles of the **alphabetic code** – linking letters and sounds, developing what is known as **grapheme–phoneme** correspondence (GPC). They can then begin to learn to read, using their GPC knowledge to decode phonically regular words and say them out loud.

Phonics for reading in the National Curriculum

The current National Curriculum (NC) framework encourages teachers to put a greater emphasis on using 'phonics' in teaching reading, and the *Letters and Sounds* programme from the DfE offers the support for delivering this. The revised NC in development for implementation in 2014 is more specific in its requirement for teaching reading using systematic synthetic phonics from the beginning of schooling through to the end of Year 2. From Year 3 phonics generally begins to become redundant as readers develop automaticity in using their phonics skills.

See Chapter 10 for further information about phonics and the older learner.

The golden rules of teaching children to decode

 Choose and stick to a teaching sequence.

 Ensure good GPC knowledge.

Provide good modelling of GPC, sound processing and blending skills.

 Provide opportunities to revise, practise and apply newly taught phonic knowledge and skills:

TOP TIP

Do it early.

Keep it simple.

Complete it by age 7.

- this means structured games and activities as well as books specifically designed cumulatively for accessibility.

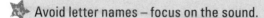 Avoid letter names – focus on the sound.

Remember sound plus sound plus sound equals a word when blended together.

Don't confuse decoding with other aspects of reading which are just as important for different reasons, e.g. sharing picture books, reading aloud to a child, listening to stories.

Have clear strategies for tricky bits (irregular and longer words, syllabification or chunking, etc.).

What is a decodable text?

The term '**decodable**' refers to words containing only the letters and sounds the child has already learned. The nature and content of a decodable text will grow with the knowledge and understanding of the child, so are not static things but are dependent upon where the child is within the sequence of learning the alphabetic code. Any core phonics programme approved by the DfE will include decodable texts.

Why are decodable texts so important?

In beginning reading, it is important that you systematically provide opportunities for children to practise and apply the phonic skills they have been taught. If a child is presented with a text that you know allows him or her to practise, this will not only ensure useful practice but will build confidence too. If you present a child with a text for independent reading which is not decodable, then the child will not be able to practise his or her skills and apply knowledge to read it. This may lead to frustration and/or cause the child to resort to incorrect strategies, e.g. guessing.

So if you provide decodable text it ensures that a child can use and develop correct print-to-sound phonic processes and skills and avoid potentially damaging bad habits.

How do you know if a text is decodable?

In order to know whether a text is decodable, you have two options:

Either trust that it is part of a published core programme and is therefore being offered as an opportunity to practise what has already systematically been taught.

Or evaluate the content in terms of the phonetic content of the vocabulary and compare it to the phonic knowledge the child has been taught.

Decodable text increases in difficulty as the children's knowledge of the alphabetic code and decoding skills develop. The checklist below can help you to decide if a text is at the right level.

> • Does it feature letter sounds the children know?
>
> • Does it feature phonetic structures the children know? E.g. they can know /a/ and /r/ but it doesn't mean they know /ar/.
>
> • Does it feature the right length of word? E.g. begin with single-syllable words and build up to words with two or more syllables. Whilst we promote strategies for tackling longer words, in the early stages CVC words will be the easiest to read.

This doesn't mean that all short words are easier to read! *Of*, *is* and *to* are very short but **tricky words** until you know the rules.

Similarly, a short book or a book that features very few words is not necessarily more easily decodable than a longer book or one that features more words. If you are using a core phonics programme, then the reading books associated with it will be decodable (bar a few **high-frequency words** which should be declared).

If you are not using a core phonics programme, then a document such as *Letters and Sounds* can help you to understand where children are in the phases of phonic development and therefore what sorts of words they will be able to decode. The document provides lists of words that you can use to create your own words, phrases, captions, sentences or even stories.

TOP TIP

Evaluate the vocabulary by structure to decide if it is decodable for a child or group of children at a particular phase of learning. Don't only rely on what is printed in a book by the publisher, or on the number of words, the length of the book, the number of pictures …

Are decodable texts void of meaning?

In the early stages, and in order to offer an effective amount of reading practice, the decodable text may be necessarily constrained in its language. But it doesn't have to stay that way! Quickly the child can move from *Pip sits on a pin* to *Tick tock went the clock* to *The star shines brightly at night* …

If a child is reading word lists of decodable words then this clearly is not a story. If you are using decodable texts, there is no reason why these should be boring or void of meaning. There are many published core programmes now available which work miracles with very few and very simple CVC words.

Some publishers provide texts for paired reading, with one side of a page meant to be read by the adult and the other side decodable for the child, like the example shown here from the Usborne First Reading series, Mairi MacKinnon's *Dog Diary* (Usborne Publishing, 2010).

Mairi MacKinnon's *Dog Diary*

In the first part of the series, adult and child take turns to read, with the child's share becoming greater and more challenging in each book. These books cover material that is normally taught during a child's first year at school.

What is the purpose of pictures in decodable texts?

The pictures in a decodable text are part of the story offering but they are not there to help the child guess the meaning of a word. Rather, the picture should add to the enjoyment of the story and support but not mirror the text. This has been a controversial point for many years, but if a child is decoding well then a picture is nice to have rather than a critical part of the experience.

There are phonics books available that deliberately only exist to provide reading practice of single words, in the same way that word cards might. They are a precursor to reading decodable stories. On the right is an example of a series like this from the publisher Get Reading Right.

The Get Reading Right resources continue with sentence books, which also provide pictures that bear no relation to the text, and then move on to decodable story books which feature artwork related to the story.

Practise Book from Get Reading Right

There are also resources and books that show nonsense words or pseudo-words. These 'made up' words usually feature with an alien or monster to try to provide a context for the children in line with the Year 1 Phonics Screening Check (see Chapter 11 for more about this).

What about books that are not decodable?

Decodable books provide appropriate practice in decoding in the early stages of learning to read, and so build confidence and ensure success in developing independence in reading. They should never replace or prevent access to a rich and diverse range of children's books.

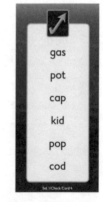

Check and Progress Phonics Cards from Rising Stars.

It is essential that all kinds of other texts are used and enjoyed using a range of other teaching methodologies for different purposes.

TOP TIP

When it's your turn to read to a child or children, there are no restrictions.

When it's the child's turn to read a text to you, select a decodable text to ensure success.

What is the connection between decoding and comprehension?

Phonics instruction helps readers to understand GPC.

GPC helps readers to decode words.

Decoding words aids and develops word recognition.

The more words recognised, the easier reading becomes.

The more opportunities there are to practise decoding and word recognition, the easier reading becomes.

Reading fluency and automaticity improve.

Reading fluency improves reading comprehension. As fluency improves so more time can be spent on vocabulary and concept demands (less time decoding; more time addressing meanings).

Ease and automaticity are liberating, so reading can be about learning and enjoyment.

> *… reading fluency is the bridge between decoding and comprehension.*
> (Marcie Penner-Wilger's *Reading Fluency: A Bridge from Decoding to Comprehension*, 2008), http://eps.schoolspecialty.com/downloads/other/acad-read/fluency_research.pdf

> *Good readers use decoding to read a word they don't know. It helps them to work it out.*
> (www.bainbridgeclass.com)

> *Good readers use comprehension strategies to make sure they understand the meaning of what they are reading.*
> (www.bainbridgeclass.com)

Is decoding subsequently redundant?

Even as proficient adult readers, we occasionally fall back on our decoding skills to read an unfamiliar word, for example:

> **dactyloscopy** *n.* comparison of fingerprints for identification.

Similarly, even when reading fluently, children should be encouraged to use a range of strategies as well as their phonic skills.

 Semantics – does it make sense?

 Syntactic/structural experience – does it sound right or does it fit with the rules I know about English?

How can readers use both decoding and comprehension skills?

We need to model for children how to make use of their decoding skills in order to engage and make sense of a text that is not written as part of a synthetic phonics programme and so may not be entirely decodable.

Just as with any transference of skills, the children need to be shown how to use and apply their phonic knowledge and skills in the real world.

This is the sort of structure we offer children in a guided reading session. We aim to give them confidence in tackling a text with more depth.

TOP TIP

Use this routine for ensuring that decoding skills are still used to facilitate comprehension when children move beyond decodable texts.

 Pre-read a text:

- What do we already know about the topic or story? This is sometimes referred to as 'activating prior knowledge'.

- Look for or discuss unfamiliar or tricky words, whether they are high-frequency words or content-related words. Apply decoding skills to read them and check their meanings. Practise blending these words and segmenting them for spelling.

- Decoding up front in this way will minimise the tendency in poorer readers to skip or substitute incorrect words.

Engage with the text:

- Focus on content, make connections, ask questions and visualise what is being read in order to understand it.

 Read the text and re-read it several times to practise fluency and to rethink meanings.

Strategy

Several online organisations and individuals produce posters to help children to remember the strategies they need to use for developing comprehension and decoding. However, you can make your own or get the children to make them just as effectively. The trick is to ensure that children see the range of strategies available to them just at the point when they need them. Readers who forget their decoding skills too quickly may become frustrated and those who stick rigidly to decoding will be slow and lose confidence and interest.

A selection of posters from Prim-Ed Publishing, which offer top tips on decoding and comprehension.

Check out www.bainbridgeclass.com/beanieposters for some initial ideas as well as those from Prim-Ed Publishing (www.prim-ed.com). While for posters offering top tips on decoding and comprehension, visit www.literacysolutions.com.au/resources/decoding-comprehension-strategies.php.

CHAPTER 9 PHONICS FOR WRITING – SPELLING

What underpins phonics for writing?

Reading and writing are different sides of the same coin:

> We blend to read using **decoding** skills. We segment to spell using encoding skills.

Synthetic phonics is built around the notion of this reversibility.

Phonics helps us to make sense of speech sounds so that we can write them down to make words.

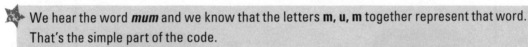

★ We hear the word *mum* and we know that the letters **m, u, m** together represent that word. That's the simple part of the code.

★ We hear the word *pharaoh* and we know that there are spelling choices to be made but that in this instance the letters **ph** are code for /f/, **ara** are code for /air/ and **oh** are code for /oa/. That's a more complex part of the code.

Even when children can read quite complex words such as *pharaoh*, they (like us) will continue to make errors in spelling those words because it's difficult to always make the right choice! Refer to the lists of words most commonly misspelt, later in this chapter.

Revisiting 'The simple view of reading' for understanding writing

Academics, teachers and the government now recognise 'The simple view of reading' model, as recommended in the *Independent Review of the Teaching of Early Reading* (2006; also known as The Rose Report). The diagram summarises the connection between language **comprehension** and word recognition, which is the core of this model (for more on this model of reading refer back to Chapter 8).

It is no surprise then that this model can be applied to writing also. Ruth Miskin does this in the Read, Write Inc. *Phonics Handbook* (Oxford University Press, 2011), which explains most of what we need to understand about writing. Miskin explains this complex process simply:

> *Children need to have both good word recall and good oral language comprehension in order to write.*
> *Good word recall is dependent upon encoding rapidly.*
> *Good oral language comprehension is dependent upon the deliberate use of talk.*
> (Ruth Miskin, Read Write Inc. *Phonics Handbook,* Oxford University Press, 2011)

What does this view mean in terms of spelling and writing skills?

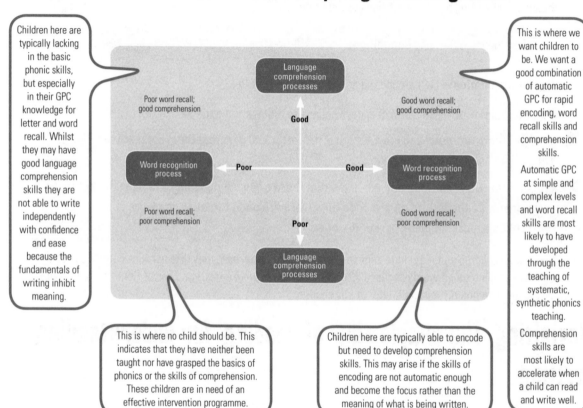

Children here are typically lacking in the basic phonic skills, but especially in their GPC knowledge for letter and word recall. Whilst they may have good language comprehension skills they are not able to write independently with confidence and ease because the fundamentals of writing inhibit meaning.

This is where we want children to be. We want a good combination of automatic GPC for rapid encoding, word recall skills and comprehension skills.

Automatic GPC at simple and complex levels and word recall skills are most likely to have developed through the teaching of systematic, synthetic phonics teaching.

Comprehension skills are most likely to accelerate when a child can read and write well.

This is where no child should be. This indicates that they have neither been taught nor have grasped the basics of phonics or the skills of comprehension. These children are in need of an effective intervention programme.

Children here are typically able to encode but need to develop comprehension skills. This may arise if the skills of encoding are not automatic enough and become the focus rather than the meaning of what is being written.

What is the role of talk?

Listening, speaking and the development of vocabulary underpin language development. The more we read, the more vocabulary we have, and the more vocabulary we have, the more we have to draw upon for understanding and writing. The more we read, the better writers we become.

What types of activities are important for teaching and practising writing?

- Identify potential tricky bits in words. Chant them in sound-talk or clap them so that the children see how to overcome the tricky bit. E.g. *mouse* – **m-ou-se**. The **-se** is no problem when you know that you have to put the **s** and **e** together to make /s/.

- Practise saying and spelling words to memorise them. Say a word, e.g. *mouse*. Say and count the phonemes for the word. Practise writing the letters for each phoneme – in the air or on each finger – as you say the sound.

- In pairs, children try writing the word and other words that share the focus 'tricky' bit. E.g. *mouse*, *house*, *louse*.

- Test if the children can write the words with the focus tricky bit. Make this part of the normal routine. Look out for children who can go on to use the correct spelling in their own writing. Transference of skills is critical.

- Mini-dictations. Choose some simple phrases or sentences that feature the focus tricky spelling. Say these as mini-dictations, repeating each one up to six times to give enough confidence for children to be able to remember the tricky spelling. Can the children remember the phrase or sentence and encode it in order to write it? Can they build in punctuation too? It's a big step, but a crucial one.

- Innovate on simple phrases and sentences. E.g. change the subject, the noun, the adverb, the adjective. Show the children how much fun there is in playing with language when decoding and encoding become more automatic.

- Can children create, remember and write their own phrases or sentences? Many children need lots of support for this step so they may work in a group, in pairs or individually. They have to remember a thought, transcribe it into words, encode each word and write it down.

- Check spellings (and punctuation). Encourage the children to check their own work or their partner's work so they understand the value of errors.

- Encourage composition. Prepare and support the children by talking about ideas, providing a reason to write, anticipating vocabulary needs, rehearsing sentences orally, asking questions, taking a modular and scaffolded approach so the children are not overwhelmed with the task and lose sight of their ideas or become frustrated.

A note about handwriting

All mainstream core synthetic phonic teaching programmes include letter formation as part of the teaching of the letters and sounds. However, the sequence for teaching the letters will reflect the order that is most supportive of phonics (e.g. **s a t p**, **i n m d**, etc.).

> This isn't a book about 'writing' – but there are many publications available about the strategies for supporting creative writing. The Talk for Writing work from Pie Corbett is particularly influential in this area (www.literacytrust.org.uk/news_blogs/email_updates/interviews/pie_corbett).

Most handwriting programmes (e.g. Gill Budgell and Kate Ruttle's *Penpals for Handwriting*, Cambridge-Hitachi, 2008) teach the letters based on the principles of letter families and similarity of letter formation. So letters are taught as:

- long ladder letters: **l, i, t, u, j, y**
- curly caterpillar letters: **c, a, d, o, s, g, q, e, f**
- one-armed robot letters: **r, b, n, h, m, k, p**
- zig-zag monster letters: **z, x, v, w.**

Handwriting schemes focus on patterns and motor control as well as fluency and legibility. Discrete handwriting lessons support on-going phonic work and are a crucial part of the daily repertoire.

Most schools teach joining the letters once the children are about age 6 or 7 and are beginning to spell with more certainty. This can work really well if it coincides with the teaching of **digraphs**, e.g. **ch**, **sh**, **ai**, **ow**, or trigraphs, e.g. **air**, **ear**, **igh**, since the movement of writing these letters joined together can, for some children, help with learning them as a phoneme. Some hands-on resources provide magnetic or sponge versions of these **graphemes** joined in this way.

Phonics Phase 5 Magnetic Letters from TTS Group.

As writing automaticity develops, handwriting remains important for improving speed and style.

The 100 most often misspelt words among 5- to 11-year-olds

There are many lists like the one shown below, and there will be some variation, but much consensus too! It's worrying to see many phonically regular words on this list; target those first.

their	to	there	they	then
your	clothes	looked	people	pretty
because	thought	and	beautiful	it's
something	named	came	name	tried
swimming	first	were	than	two
let's	mother	another	through	some
woman	animals	started	that's	would
said	wanted	bear	from	frightened
cousin	alright	happened	didn't	always
interesting	sometimes	friends	children	an
until	our	asked	off	through
running	believe	little	things	him
went	where	stopped	very	morning
here	many	know	with	together
now	decided	friend	money	when
its	bought	getting	going	course
again	heard	received	coming	too
for	February	once	like	they're
surprise	before	caught	every	different
school	jumped	around	dropped	babies

The following may cause problems:

⭐ **High-frequency words**, e.g. **and** is frequently used and phonically regular ... but still is on the list. These words need to be explicitly taught and practised.

⭐ Homophones, e.g. *they*, *they're*, *their* or *there*.

⭐ Double-letter combinations, e.g. *dropped*, *happened*, *running*, *getting*.

⭐ Compound words, e.g. *something*, *sometimes*.

Top 20 misspelt words in the UK:

1. separate
2. definitely
3. manoeuvre
4. embarrass
5. occurrence
6. consensus
7. unnecessary
8. acceptable
9. broccoli
10. referred
11. bureaucracy
12. supersede
13. questionnaire
14. connoisseur
15. a lot
16. entrepreneur
17. particularly
18. liquify/liquefy
19. conscience
20. parallel

Source: www. OnePoll.com, which carried out the study of 3,500 Britons in 2010.

- Unstressed **vowels** or the *schwa* sound, e.g. ***cousin*** where the **i** is unstressed, ***together*** where the **er** at the end is unstressed, ***again*** where the initial **a** is unstressed – see note about *schwa* on page 81.

- Apostrophes, e.g. ***it's*** or ***let's***.

- Confusables, e.g. ***bought/brought***, ***until/till***, ***through/thorough***.

- Less publicised pairings of 'two letters but one sound' – often known as silent letters, e.g. ***know***, ***when***, ***knight*** but also ***February***, ***people***, ***friend***.

- Past tense endings, e.g. ***jumped*** where the final **ed** is pronounced as /t/, ***looked*** where the final **ed** is pronounced as /d/, ***decided*** where the final **ed** is pronounced as /id/.

- Letters behaving differently from their norm, e.g. **o** as /u/ in ***money***, **o** as /i/ in ***women***, **o** as /w/ in ***once***, **ow** in ***know*** and ***how***, etc.

Other classic areas of difficulty

These include:

- prefixes, e.g. ***unnecessary, misspelt, antifreeze***

- suffixes and word endings, e.g. **-able** and **-ible** in ***acceptable, terrible***; **-ance** and **–ence** in ***independence, ambulance***

- polysyllabic words, e.g. ***temperature, misunderstanding***

- **c** and **s**, e.g. ***cousin, necessary, Christmas, city, cycle, science***

- **g** and **j**, e.g. ***game, Gill, magic, badge***

- **wa** where the **a** is often pronounced as /o/, e.g. ***want, wash, was***

- spellings of /or/

- spellings of long /oo/.

> The phoneme /or/ may be represented by at least 12 different spellings:
> or – ***fork***, aw – ***yawn***, our – ***pour***, au – ***audio***, al – ***stalk***, oar – ***boar***, oor – ***poor***, ore – ***core***, augh – ***taught***, ough – ***thought***, ar – ***war***, a – ***water***.

> The phoneme long /oo/ may be represented by at least eight different spellings:
> oo – ***moon***, ue – ***blue***, ew – ***blew***, o – ***move***, ou – ***soup***, ough – ***through***, u-e – ***June***, u – ***super***.

A note about *schwa*

Schwa is taken from the Hebrew word *sewa* meaning nought, as in 'there is no vowel sound'. We understand it to represent the unstressed syllable in a word with a quick **uh** sound; it is closest in sound to /u/.

Like other aspects of phonics and pronunciation issues, *schwa* can vary according to regional pronunciation, but here are some basic facts about where it usually appears. The *schwa*:

* only features in words of more than one syllable

* is never pronounced on the stressed syllable, e.g. **_normal_**

* rarely replaces a long vowel sound

* usually shows up in polysyllabic words.

TOP TIP

If you can cross out a **vowel** sound without changing the pronunciation then it's probably going to be a *schwa*, e.g. **camel** is not /c//a//m//e//l/ but /c//a//m//l/ so the /e/ is a *schwa* /uh/.

The following chart shows examples of *schwa* in simple and **tricky words**, representing different short vowel sounds.

Vowel:	a at the beginning of a word	a at the end of a word	e in a word	i in a word	o in a word	u in a word
Simple word	*away*	*canal*	*camel*	*pupil*	*lemon*	*focus*
Trickier words	*annoyed* *atishoo*	*formal* *umbrella*	*budget* *centre* *teacher*	*cousin* *pencil*	*carrot* *thorough* *flavour*	*circus* *succeed*

What about spelling rules?

We can teach the rules and/or encourage children to discover them. Educational views tend to swing back and forth on which is most engaging and more effective. The truth is that both are important; some rules are worth discovering and some are worth being told. Some rules may take a lifetime to discover. *Letters and Sounds* Phase 6 suggests that children are taught spelling conventions and guidelines to develop their knowledge of the spelling system.

Letters and Sounds Phase 6 suggests the teaching of:
* the past tense
* adding suffixes – **ing**, **ed**, **er**, **est**, **fully** and **y**
* long words
* finding and learning the tricky bits in words
* adding **s** and **es** to nouns and verbs.

The revised National Curriculum is almost certainly going to require systematic teaching of spelling, grammar and punctuation, as reflected in the additional Standard Assessment Task at the end of Key Stage 2.

CHAPTER 10 PHONICS ... AND OLDER LEARNERS

What you need to know

Children who have not mastered the basic skills of **decoding** by age 6 need a fast-track rewind course to ensure that they do not slip further behind. Children not reading with a degree of confidence in word recognition by age 7 need intervention strategies to help them to catch up. Children who finish primary school not being able to read fluently will encounter difficulties in keeping up with the demands of the curriculum in secondary school. And too many of our students are facing that difficulty. Too many children in Key Stage 2 and above (and adults) fall into this category.

Some of these older learners may have special needs of one kind or another, whether social, developmental, physical or cultural. They must learn to crack the **alphabetic code** in order to read, so that they can read to learn. We will not deal here with severe special needs that need expert intervention but rather with the vast majority of those who experience difficulties that can fairly easily be overcome.

> Older readers often have to shake off bad habits and ineffective strategies and begin to learn to read again using very small but quick steps and specific phonic knowledge and skills.

Types of older reader

Beginners

These readers have not cracked the alphabetic code so they have poor **phoneme–grapheme** correspondence and word recognition skills, and begin to rely on visual and context cues to 'guess' at words.

Stuck on simple reading readers

These readers have cracked the simple aspects of the alphabetic code but not the more complex aspects of it (e.g. they may know /ay/ can be represented by a range of spellings such as **ai** and **a-e** but they could be easily confused when they hit **ey** as in *grey* or **eigh** as in *sleigh*). They may not have strategies to attack longer words. So, whilst they can manage with simple material, they struggle with the more complex texts involved in reading to learn. They compensate by devising complex survival strategies which involve relying on **sight-words** and guessing from pictures and context clues.

Stilted readers

These readers have cracked the alphabetic code but have not mastered enough to have reached automaticity. Reading is slow and stilted so it is frustrating, **comprehension** suffers and motivation is lacking. These children need practice, practice, practice to reboot their confidence, remind them of the purposes of reading and reignite their enthusiasm.

Late readers

These readers may have caught up and have automatic word recognition skills and be able to use decoding strategies, but as they acquired these skills later they are lacking in comprehension skills and strategies. They become 'reluctant' readers because they feel left behind; confidence and motivation are problems.

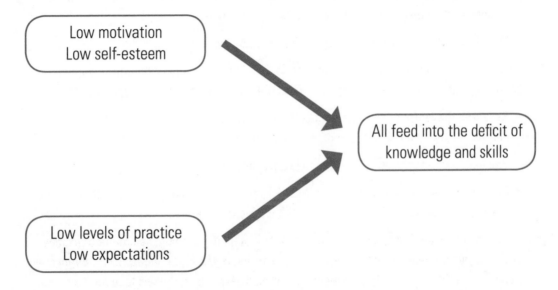

A photocopiable checklist for profiling a reader's specific difficulties is provided on page 90.

The children with specific needs such as **dyslexia**, children learning English as a second (or third) language or those who have no apparent reason for having missed the 'reading boat' the first time around may be in any of these categories. There will also be many other categories; this is not a science but just one way to think about where different learners are on the reading spectrum and how best to help them to fast forward.

What are some of the particular challenges for older learners learning English as an additional language?

TOP TIP

Use COGNATES!

These are words in two different languages that share a similar meaning, spelling and pronunciation, for example:

- English *gorilla*/Spanish *gorila*
- English *three*/Polish *trzy*, cat/ *kot*.

After Key Stage 1 **phonics** is less specifically taught, so any help in Key Stage 2 will be catch-up/intervention, at secondary school, when phonics is not part of the curriculum.

- Find ways to build a school policy to support these learners across the curriculum; this is never easy but it is essential. Phonics can be integrated into content and classroom lessons and texts as well as into vocabulary instruction.

- If possible, arrange intensive intervention or catch-up.

Some learners may not have learned to read in their first language or their first language may not be phonetic, so they may struggle to grasp the relationship between letters and sounds.

- Research the learners' first languages to understand the skills they bring to the classroom and to build on these in teaching and learning to make connections.

- Use hands-on resources to help teach letters and sounds.

- Give plenty of time and support to learners whose first language is not left to right, e.g. Arabic, or is not sound based but symbol based, e.g. Japanese.

Lack of vocabulary and comprehension may further impede learning, as connections may not be obvious or meaningful (or useful!). E.g. learning *night*, *sight*, *flight*, *fright*, *plight* may be useful for stressing the /igh/ phoneme, but which of these words will be useful on a day-to-day basis for a language learner new to English?

- Select vocabulary carefully.

Resources are often aimed at younger children so these are at best a turn-off and at worst a total turn-off. Older learners have more sophisticated experiences of life and language and can use higher-order thinking skills resources which younger learners will not expect.

- Ensure that material is age-appropriate, look for high-interest texts with a low reading age and teach phonics in context to retain interest.

What is catch-up?

Catch-up programmes are specifically designed to engage learners who have not mastered the basics of reading and spelling, and to quickly ensure that they recover and continue their learning at an appropriate level of mainstream education.

Catch-up programmes should be flexible to meet the differing needs of the learners.

- Identify the difficulty/needs as early as possible.
- Involve highly skilled teachers and specialists.
- Work in partnerships with colleagues and parents as appropriate.
- Plan an intensive but short campaign.
- Review and adapt the campaign frequently.
- Measure success.

What catch-up resources are available?

In the DfE online listing of resources, *New Pro5 Phonics Catalogue,* the following programmes are cited as being suitable for catch-up at Key Stage 1, and many are suitable for older learners too:

- *Phonics Bug* published by Pearson. Guidance is provided in *Teaching and Assessment Guides.*
- *Phonics International* by Debbie Hepplewhite (available at www.phonicsinternational.com/guidance_book.pdf).
- *Sound Discovery®* by Anne Kathryn and Marlynne Grant, published by Ridgehill Publishing, provides placement tests, teaching lesson plans and review lessons.
- *One-to-One Phonics Tutoring Kit* by Ruth Miskin, published by Oxford University Press. Or try Read Write Inc. *Fresh Start: Modules and Anthology* by Ruth Miskin and Tim Archbold (Oxford University Press, 2011).

(www.pro5.org/en/news_press/870/News-New-Pro5-Phonics-Catalogue)

There are hundreds of intervention and catch-up programmes to choose from, so assess these against the DfE core criteria and the checklist of features later in this chapter.

What types of supplementary resources and specific skill resources are useful?

All core programmes that are suitable for catch-up will offer the full range of resource types for reviewing, teaching, practising, applying and assessing. However, supplementary programmes and games exist too. In addition to the rigour of the teaching sequence, motivation is hugely important, so a rich range of resource types is also important. Some examples include:

trugs from Read Successfully.

- trugs: a series of **decodable** card games to practise, reinforce and consolidate phonics, available from Read Successfully (www. readsuccessfully.com).

- Phonicshark: a computer program by White Shark (http://wordshark. co.uk) for teaching **synthetic phonics**.

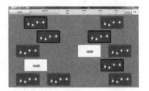

A screenshot from Phonicshark a phonics teaching program.

What features are important for a catch-up programme?

- Systematic core resources for learning the basic grapheme–**phoneme** correspondences to automaticity.

- Differentiated opportunities for **blending** and **segmenting** at word, sentence and text level.

- VAK (visual, auditory and kinaesthetic) resources.

- Opportunities for flexible learning and over-learning.

- Facilities to print material in different font sizes, colours and sequences for personalised learning and/or small groups.

What catch-up training is available?

Training can range from a single day up to about 3 days and may be linked to a published programme or be generic. Training organisations regarded as offering specific catch-up training by literacy specialists are listed below. This list will change over time but serves as a guide.

- CfBT Education Trust
- Debbie Hepplewhite
- Osiris Educational Ltd
- Rising Stars UK Ltd – Sound Reading System

- Ruth Miskin Literacy Ltd
- Sounds-Write Ltd
- Teach to Read
- Which Phonics

Phonics across the curriculum

How can we support older learners across the curriculum?

Establish core principles across subjects in the following areas:

- Language: agree which terms will be used across all subjects when referring to phonics, e.g. phonemes, graphemes, blending, segmenting.

- Displays: create **mnemonics** for each subject, create an alphabetic code chart with vocabulary relevant to each subject, create a bank of subject-specific pictures for spelling practice, e.g. *test tube*, create displays of words with phonic clues for reading, e.g.: *temperature* – **tem-per-a-ture**, *addition* – **a-dd-i-tion**.

- Techniques: agree which techniques will be used across all subjects when referring to phonics, e.g. **sound-talk**, making learning active, guided reading, paired reading, talk for writing, giving 'phonic time' (time to work out a word).

- A school-wide approach to **tricky words**.

- Types of activities that work and are common and/or those that work for specific subjects.

- Sharing good practice: set up an online notice board, using www.wallwisher.com or similar to share good practice with colleagues. Set one up for the children too.

- Multimedia: allow students to prepare audio instructions or short videos to remind themselves of the stages in a procedure – put them online or on the intranet.

The following shows a collection of ideas for the implementation of phonics across the curriculum with older learners.

Group challenge for tricky vocabulary	**Mnemonics** and rules in every class	'Word of the week' for each subject	Key words for topics for reading and spelling
Phonics first approach – give it a go, then ask or check	Use colour coding for tricky bits in words	'Snap', 'Happy Families', 'Bingo' across subjects	Use phoneme frames
Use syllables	Use sound-talk	Involve students in making audio recordings or short films	Use modelling dough to physically build letters/words.
Make learning active	Play word games, e.g. add, decimal, lines, square	Range of reading approaches; group, guided, buddy, paired	Use incidental opportunites, e.g. x, y axes, isosceles.

A model lesson plan

Can your lessons incorporate the following elements?

★ Review – always check previous learning.

★ Visual literacy for vocabulary, comprehension, speaking and listening – use pictures for discussion to tune children in and activate prior knowledge.

★ Phonics for reading – ensure there are opportunities for teaching, practising and applying blending skills, decoding and developing independence and fluency.

★ Phonics for writing – ensure there are opportunities for teaching, practising and applying segmenting skills, encoding and developing independence and automaticity.

★ Listening skills – check aural skills and don't forget the usefulness of aural comprehension.

★ Check – always check that the teaching has been effective with a check or test, whether informal or formal.

Resources to support the transition from learning to read to reading to learn

Once learners achieve a functional level of literacy, how can we best move them on to wider reading whilst supporting their newly found phonic skills?

It is important to choose 'next-step' resources carefully – pay attention to readability in terms of:

★ decodable words

★ punctuation

★ amount of text

★ content of text

★ grammar

★ vocabulary

★ layout of text

★ role of illustration.

There is a rich range of reading material now available for the struggling or reluctant older reader including fiction, non-fiction, plays in mini-series or whole programmes as well as in print and on-screen.

A selection of mini-series targeting the older learner, available from Rising Stars.

The Project X CODE series is available from Oxford University Press and is useful for older learners and as a phonics-based intervention for children from Year 2.

The Rapid Phonics series is available from Pearson Eduction

Useful links

- Cumbria University online support – https://portfolio.pebblepad.co.uk/cumbria/

- Catch Up Literacy – www.catchup.org/ a 'not-for-profit' charity which addresses the problems of underachievement in literacy and numeracy through training and resources. Not solely phonic focused.

- Literacy Trust – www.literacytrust.org.uk/

- *What Works for Pupils with Literacy Difficulties? The Effectiveness of Intervention Schemes* by Greg Brooks, University of Sheffield, available from www.nieku.com/~spld/assets/documents/Greg-Brooks.pdf

Checklist to identify the specific nature of reading difficulties

Difficulty ...	Yes/No/Notes
Reading at pace: • With pauses • With stumbles/hesitations • With robot stress and/or intonation • With repeat errors • Breaks for high-frequency or tricky words • Loses place • Skips words/lines • Too fast with errors • Other	
Remembering: • Letter–sound relationships • Words • Phrases, sentences • Sequences/directions • Other	
Thinking: • Order • Logic • Other	
Blending right through a word: • Uses first or last letter and guesses • Reverses letter order when blending • Guesses • Other	

Difficulty ...	Yes/No/Notes
Segmenting to spell: • Uses first or last letter and guesses • Reverses letter order when segmenting • Guesses • Other	
Writing: • Cannot copy accurately • Incorrect letter formation • Poor or illegible handwriting • Other	
Comprehension: • Understanding words • Understanding sentences • Understanding instruction • Higher-level skill (e.g. inference) • Other	
Emotions: • Distracted by ... • Short attention span • Withdrawn • Anxious • Other	
Physical: • Auditory discrimination • Visual discrimination • Oral production • Kinaesthetic • Other	

CHAPTER 11 TESTING AND CHECKS

Introduction

In the past, when teachers taught **phonics** the assessment was school-based, as there was no statutory assessment test in common use.

As the interest in and importance of phonics as a critical part of our teaching in the early years have increased in our schools, so has the number of resources available to support the teaching and assessment of the core skills of phonics. So now we find:

- core phonics programmes that offer guidance on assessment or substantial assessment strands
- assessment guidance after each of *Letters and Sounds* Phases 2–5
- phonics included in National Curriculum Key Stage 1
- a Year 1 Phonics Screening Check
- resources for schools provided by local education authorities.

The Year 1 Phonics Screening Check means that children aged 6 will now be assessed in basic phonic skills (see later in this chapter for more information on the check).

When does the assessment of phonics take place?

Ideally, the assessment of phonics is on-going and informal in most classrooms, and takes place during the daily phonics session.

Revisit and review
Note which children respond confidently when practising previously learned **graphemes** and/or **blending** and **segmenting**.

Teach
Assess how well the children respond to teaching of new graphemes or **tricky words** and whether they make links with previous learning when appropriate.

Practise
Note how well the children engage in partner work and whether they demonstrate growing

confidence in their use of the new grapheme. Note how successfully they practise blending and/or segmenting words with the new grapheme—**phoneme** correspondence.

Apply

Note how well the children are able to apply independently what they have just been taught, as well as what they know and remember from previous sessions, as they read or write captions/sentences containing the new skills and knowledge.

Assess learning against criteria

Record significant observations in a simple way so that they effectively inform next steps in teaching and learning. As well as on-going classroom assessment, there are also more summative assessments available and also a statutory one (see information below about the Phonics Screening Check for 6-year-olds).

What is Ofsted looking for when inspecting reading?

Whilst Ofsted is now charged more directly with inspecting early reading, it is clear that phonics is just one part of this new focus. Assessments at the end of the Early Years Foundation Stage (EYFS) and at the end of Key Stage 1 will only show part of the picture. Children's fluency, enjoyment, knowledge of books and authors, and alternative strategies used for **decoding** are all equally important areas to explore. Phonics is a means to an end, and never an end in itself.

In its inspection of quality of provision and outcomes for reading, Ofsted look at the following aspects:

- evidence gathering
- identifying children who are falling through the net
- systems and leadership
- assessment, grouping and intervention
- expectations
- high-quality phonic work
- teaching the higher levels of phonics (complex code)
- listening to children reading.

> The assessment of individual pupil's progress, phonic knowledge and skills is sufficiently frequent and detailed to identify quickly the pupils who are falling behind or in danger of failing to keep up with their peers. Effective provision for them to catch up is put in place early and there are high expectations of what all pupils should achieve.
>
> (Ofsted, *Reading by Six: How the Best Schools do It*, 2010. Available from www.ofsted.gov.uk/resources/reading-six-how-best-schools-do-it)

(Ofsted, Module 4: Inspecting quality, *Getting them Reading Early*, 2011)

What does assessment look like in the Early Years Foundation Stage 2012?

The EYFS includes the requirement to complete a profile for each child aged 3–5 years against the Early Learning Goals of the EYFS and to complete this by the end of Reception.

In terms of literacy and phonics in particular, this means that children will be scored in the areas as shown on page 61 of Chapter 7.

What support is there in *Letters and Sounds*?

Letters and Sounds offers assessment guidance at the end of each phase. This guidance is outlined in the following pages.

It is important to remember that boundaries between the phases should not be seen as fixed. For example, some children will be introduced to Phase 3 graphemes before they are secure at Phase 2, while continuing to practise the skills of blending and segmentation. Similarly, some children will learn to blend and segment words containing adjacent **consonants** during Phases 2 or 3, rather than waiting until Phase 4. Remember, phonics is not a science and children's learning will ebb and flow just as it does in any other area of the curriculum. Learning is not a perfect curve.

End of Phase 2

Phase 2 teaches children at least 19 new graphemes and should move them on from oral blending and segmenting to working on these skills with letters. Phase 2 should take about 6 weeks.

Are the children working securely with these new skills?

Children should be able to:

 Say the sound when shown any of these graphemes:

Set 1:	**s**	**a**	**t**	**p**
Set 2:	**i**	**n**	**m**	**d**
Set 3:	**g**	**o**	**c**	**k**
Set 4 :	**ck**	**e**	**u**	**r**
Set 5:	**h**	**b**	**f, ff**	**l, ll**	**ss**

Find any of the above graphemes from a display or selection. So, for example, you may display six plastic letters and ask a child to show you a specific letter that represents the sound /f/.

TOP TIP

You may choose to write the grapheme or use other resources such as magnetic plastic or foam letters or grapheme cards.

Orally blend CVC words.

This is a continuation of the **sound-talk** from Phase 1, which you may have practised with a toy or puppet, e.g. *I don't understand what Spot is trying to say to me. Can you help? What is his favourite colour? He is saying r-e-d. What is his favourite colour? It's red! Well done!*

You can ask the children to respond by saying the word they hear in sound-talk or by pointing to a picture of the word they hear. You will need an assessment response sheet something like the one shown below. Change the words and increase the number of words up to a maximum of ten if you wish.

TOP TIP

What you can say

(Use a set of phoneme fans, or phonemes on cards or on the board.)

- /fffff/. Find me the letter that makes that sound. Listen again … /ffff/.

Name	Date
Word to be spoken by adult.	Record the child's response. Tick if the child says the correct phonemes for the word in sound-talk. If incorrect, try to record the exact nature of the error.
1. s-u-n	
2. r-o-ck	
3. m-a-p	
4. d-o-g	
5. k-i-ss	
6. b-e-d	
7. f-a-n	
8. s-u-n-s-e-t	

 Orally segment CVC words. Again, this is a continuation of the sound-talk practised in Phase 1, but here the children are expected to speak in sound-talk. You will need an assessment response sheet like the one below. Change the words and increase the number of words up to a maximum of ten if you wish.

TOP TIP

What you can say

- It's your turn to speak in sound-talk like Spot. If I say **tip**, how does Spot say it for us?
  He says t-i-p.
- How does he say the word **dog**?

Name	Date
Word to be spoken by adult.	Record the child's response. Tick if the child says the correct phonemes for the word in sound-talk. If incorrect, try to record the exact nature of the error.
1. *Mog*	
2. *fin*	
3. *hop*	
4. *ten*	
5. *doll*	
6. *sock*	
7. *huff*	
8. *bun*	

Orally blend and segment to read and spell VC words such as *if*, *am*, *at*, *on*, *in* and pseudo-words such as *ub*, *id*, *aff*.

Some children may not be able to blend and segment CVC words by the end of Phase 2, but as long as they can do this orally and have good GPC knowledge then they are considered to be secure and may progress to Phase 3.

When assessing the skill of blending, you will need an assessment response sheet like the one below. Change the words and increase the number of words up to a maximum of ten if you wish.

Name	Date	
Example words and pseudo-words to be read by the child.	Saying the sound for each grapheme. Record the child's response.	Reading each word. Record the child's response.
1. *an*		
2. *it*		
3. *off*		
4. *at*		
5. *ob*		
6. *het*		
7. *cug*		
8. *veck*		

Note: For more about pseudo-words, see page 71 of this book.

⭐ If you want to check the child's ability to segment in order to spell, use the same sort of words as above but say the whole word for the child to segment each sound and then write a grapheme for each in order to spell the word.

⭐ Read five tricky words: *the*, *to*, *I*, *no*, *go*.

⭐ Refer to Chapter 4 for activity ideas with high-frequency and tricky words. Once you have taught these using a phonics first approach, check that the children know these words using word cards or letters. Keep a record of which tricky words each child can read and eventually spell.

End of Phase 3

Phase 3 teaches children another 25 graphemes and they further develop their skills of blending and segmenting. This phase should take about 12 weeks.

Are the children working securely with these new skills?

Children should be able to:

⭐ Give the sound when shown any of the Phase 2 graphemes (see page 93) and any of these from Phase 3:

Set 6:	**j**	**v**	**w**	**x**

Set 6:   **j**   **v**   **w**   **x**

Set 7:   **y**   **z, zz**   **qu**

Plus: **ch, sh, th** (*thin* and *this*), **ng, ai, ee, igh, oav oo** (*book* and *boot*), **ar, or, ur, ow** (*cow*), **oi, ear, air, ure** (*sure*), **er** (*corner*).

⭐ Find any of the above graphemes from a display or selection. So, for example, you may display plastic letters and ask a child to show you a specific letter or group of letters that represents the sound /air/. You may try this with the whole class, small groups or individual children. It could be it helpful to get the children to work in pairs.

TOP TIP

What you can say

(Use a set of phoneme fans, or phonemes on cards or on the board.)

• /air/. Find me the letter or groups of letters that make that sound. Listen again … /air/.

 Blend and read CVC words using the Phases 2 and 3 graphemes. You will need an assessment response sheet like the one below. Change the words and increase the number of words up to a maximum of ten if you wish.

Name	Date	
Example words and pseudo-words to be read by the child.	Saying the sound for each grapheme. Record the child's response.	Reading each word. Record the child's response.
1. wait		
2. fork		
3. hang		
4. pow		
5. zeng		
6. vigh		
7. gair		
8. yar		

 Segment and spell CVC words using the Phases 2 and 3 graphemes. If you want to check the child's ability to segment to spell, use the same sort of words as above but say the whole word for the child to segment each sound and then write a grapheme for each in order to spell the word.

Similarly, you may provide a simple picture so the child identifies the word and then segments it before spelling the whole word.

You will need to prepare a response sheet and have the children write on a separate piece of paper. At the end of the check you can staple your sheet and the child's together to add to your bank of evidence/records. Something like the chart below should suffice. Change the words and increase the number of words up to a maximum of ten if you wish.

TOP TIP

What you can say

• It's your turn to write now .

• If I say **chin**. How do you write the word **chin**?

We write **ch-i-n , chin**!

• How will you write the word **ship**? You try.

Name	Date
Example words to read aloud or picture to show the child.	Notes on the child's attempt.
1. *yak*	
2. *quick*	
3. *zip*	
4. *chain*	
5. *vish*	
6. *soit*	
7. *bax*	
8. *thoo*	

Note: It's tricky to be sure that a child is working securely but at the end of Phase 3 children must be able to make a really sensible and plausible attempt at writing a phoneme (even if it's the wrong choice). For example, if a child writes **sigh** as **sie**, that demonstrates an understanding of the alphabetic code and what is possible, it's just that in this instance the wrong choice was made. However, if a child writes **seer**, this suggests that the /igh/ phoneme is not yet secure in spelling.

Read the tricky words: *he*, *she*, *we*, *me*, *be*, *was*, *my*, *you*, *her*, *they*, *all*, *are*.

Refer to Chapter 4 for activity ideas for reading tricky words. Once you have taught these using a phonics first approach, check that the children know these words using word cards or letters. Keep a record of which tricky words each child can read and eventually spell.

Spell the tricky words: *the*, *to*, *I*, *no*, *go*.

Ask the child to write each word in response to your saying it.

Write each letter correctly when following a model. Most core programmes offer a writing model for the children to follow. Many of these are animated if they are part of a resource for the interactive whiteboard.

Alternatively, many handwriting schemes also offer guidance on correct letter formation.

The preferred style of handwriting in schools differs widely. However, most schools teach the children to write each letter with an exit flick (ready for joining letters when they are older). Some schools teach curly loops on letters for the same reason and some schools teach joined writing from the very beginning. You can only assess what has been taught, so check whether your chosen phonics programme or handwriting programme offers guidance.

You can assess children's letter formation skills by either watching their writing in a segmenting/spelling check or in a specific handwriting test in which you present a grapheme and ask the child to then write it correctly.

End of Phase 4

Phase 4 allows children to consolidate their phonic knowledge and teaches how to blend and segment words featuring adjacent consonants as well as longer words. This phase should take about 4–6 weeks.

Are the children working securely with these new skills?

Children should be able to:

- Give the sound when shown any of the Phases 2 or 3 graphemes (see previous pages).

- Find any of the Phases 2 or 3 graphemes from a display or selection, when given the sound.

- Blend and read words containing adjacent consonants and using the Phases 2 and 3 graphemes. You will need an assessment response sheet something like the one below. Change the words and increase the number of words up to a maximum of ten if you wish.

Name	Date	
Example words and pseudo-words to be read by the child.	Saying the sound for each grapheme. Record the child's response.	Reading each word. Record the child's response.
1. *tilt*		
2. *chimp*		
3. *drop*		
4. *spoon*		
5. *brint*		
6. *threb*		
7. *flonk*		
8. *sanwich*		

 Segment and spell words featuring adjacent consonants and using the Phases 2 and 3 graphemes.

If you want to check the child's ability to segment to spell, use the same sort of words as above but say the whole word for the child to segment each sound and then write a grapheme for each in order to spell the word.

Similarly, you may provide a simple picture so the child identifies the word and then segments it before spelling the whole word.

You will need to prepare a response sheet and have the children write on a separate piece of paper. At the end of the check you can staple your sheet and the child's together to add to your bank of evidence/records. Something like the chart below should suffice. Change the words and increase the number of words up to a maximum of ten if you wish.

TOP TIP

What you can say

- It's your turn to write now.
- If I say **paint**, how do you write the word **paint**?
  We write **p-ai-n-t, paint**!
- How will you write the word **steep**? You try.

Name	Date
Example words to read aloud or picture to show the child.	Notes on the child's attempt.
1. blob	
2. grin	
3. joint	
4. coast	
5. handstand	
6. treaf	
7. splank	
8. brarsh	

Note: Even though some spellings won't yet be entirely accurate, the children should have enough letter knowledge and segmenting skills to make good attempts at spelling unknown words.

 Read the tricky words: *some, one, said, come, do, so, were, when, have, there, out, like, little* and *what*.

Refer to Chapter 4 for further ideas. Once you have taught these using a phonics first approach, check that the children know these words using word cards or letters. Keep a record of which tricky words each child can read and eventually spell.

 Spell the tricky words: *he, she, we, me, be, was, my, you, her, they, all, are*.
Ask the child to write each word in response to your saying it.

 The children should now usually be able to write each letter with correct letter formation.

End of Phase 5

Phase 5 teaches alternative pronunciations for known graphemes, and new graphemes with alternative pronunciations. Children learn to make spelling choices, and how to blend and segment words featuring adjacent consonants as well as longer words.

This should continue throughout Year 1, so lasts around 30 weeks. In the summer term children will sit the Year 1 Phonics Screening Check, which checks up on their cumulative bank of phonics skills.

Are the children working securely with these new skills?

The children should be able to:

- Give the sound when shown any grapheme that has been taught.

- Write the most common graphemes for any phonemes.

- Use a phonics first approach to reading and spelling unfamiliar words, even when they are not entirely **decodable**.

- Read and spell phonically decodable polysyllabic words, e.g. ***mountains***, ***frightening***. When assessing the skill of reading you will need an assessment response sheet something like the one shown below. Change the words and increase the number of words up to a maximum of 15 if you wish.

Name	Date	
Example words to be read by the child.	Saying the sound for each grapheme. Record the child's response.	Reading each word. Record the child's response.
1. *beans*		
2. *noises*		
3. *sold*		
4. *bird*		
5. *flying*		
6. *kitchen*		
7. *elephants*		
8. *thirteen*		
9. *acrobats*		
10. *punishment*		

If you want to check a child's ability to segment to spell, use the same sort of words as above but say the whole word for the child to segment each sound and write a grapheme for each in order to spell the word.

Similarly, you may provide a simple picture so the child identifies the word and then segments it before spelling the whole word.

You will need to prepare a response sheet and have the children write on a separate piece of paper. At the end of the check you can staple your sheet and the child's together to add to your bank of evidence/records. Something like the chart below should suffice. Change the words and increase the number of words up to a maximum of 15 if you wish.

Name	Date
Example words to read aloud or picture to show the child.	Notes on the child's attempt.
1. *tissue*	
2. *value*	
3. *launch*	
4. *money*	
5. *woke*	
6. *kind*	
7. *afternoon*	
8. *breakfast*	
9. *chemist*	
10. *danger*	

Note: Even though some spellings won't yet be entirely accurate the children should have good enough letter knowledge and segmenting skills to make good attempts at spelling unknown words. The children may also now be presented with phrases and/or sentences to read and spell.

 Recognise and use the phoneme /zh/ as in **television**, **beige**, **leisure** and **casual**. Ensure you include words featuring this phoneme in assessments.

 Read automatically all 100 **high-frequency words** listed on page 34 of this book and in *Letters and Sounds*.

 Spell most of the words in the same list accurately.

 Write with correct letter formation.

The Year 1 Phonics Screening Check

This is a statutory check to be used in all maintained schools in England from 2012 and the results will be published on RAISEonline, which provides interactive analysis of school and pupil performance data.

The results will not be published in performance tables but the data will be used as follows:

- Schools may use the results to inform parents about their child's progress in developing word reading skills.

- National results will be used to track standards over time.

- National and local authority results will be reported to allow schools to benchmark the performance of their children.

Phonics Screening Check fact file

- The Phonics Screening Check is designed to confirm whether individual children have learned phonic decoding to an appropriate standard.

- Children who do not achieve the appropriate standard/score will receive intervention support from their school to catch up and will re-take the Check the following year.

- The Check comprises a list of 40 words that the children read one-to-one with a teacher. The list of words is a combination of both real and pseudo-words. Using pseudo-words allows a focus purely on decoding using phonics.
The pseudo-words will be shown to the children alongside pictures of little monsters so they are less likely to try to match the pseudo-word to their vocabulary.

The Check is useful for:

- identifying the children who may be struggling with phonic decoding early on and who need some speedy help to catch up

- pinpointing particular aspects of phonics, e.g. split **digraphs**, that a whole class found difficult, suggesting that teaching needs to be improved

- providing a benchmark against which teacher assessments may be compared and modified if necessary.

For further information see www.aaia.org.uk/am/primary/year-1-phonics-screening-check/. Sample material on the website contains information on the structure and content of the Phonics Screening Check. It contains practice words and shows how the pseudo-words in the Check will be illustrated with pictures of imaginary creatures.

There is also a video (http://vimeo.com/39441143), which offers guidance on how to score the children's attempts.

The Phonics Screening Check has two sections, as follows.

Section 1

The words in section 1 will have a variety of simple word structures (e.g. CVC, VCC, CCVC and CVCC) using single letters (**a, b, c, d, e, f, g, h, I, j, k, l, m, n, o, p, q(u), r, s, t, u, v, w, x, y, z**), some consonant digraphs (**ch, ck, ff, ll, ng, sh, ss, th, zz**) and frequent and consistent **vowel** digraphs (**ar, ee, oi, oo, or**).

Section 2

The words in section 2 will have a variety of more complex word structures (e.g. CCVCC, CCCVC, CCCVCC and two-syllable words) with some additional consonant digraphs (**ph, wh**), some less frequent and consistent vowel digraphs, including split digraphs (**a-e, ai, au, aw, ay, ea, e-e, er, ew, i-e, ie, ir, oa, o-e, ou, ow, oy, ue, u-e, ur**) and trigraphs (**air, igh**).

Commercial phonics checks and tests

Each DfE approved core programme will include an element of assessment or check. The list of approved core programmes can be viewed at www.education.gov.uk/schools/teachingandlearning/pedagogy/b00198579/phonics-products-and-the-self-assessment-process.

Phonics Check and Progress

An example of a supplementary stand-alone classroom check resource is Louise Glasspoole's *Phonics Check and Progress* (Rising Stars, 2012).

This resource consists of two packs, one for Reception which covers *Letters and Sounds* Phases 2–4 and one for Year 1 which covers *Letters and Sounds* Phases 4 and 5. It is in line with the requirements of the Year 1 Phonics Screening Check and additionally offers a check for assessing a child's ability to segment to spell.

It is easy to administer in about 6 minutes and is intended to support teachers to better understand a child's phonic skills as well as to support areas of weakness with targeted follow-up activities.

Phonics and Early Reading Assessment

Phonics and Early Reading Assessment (Pera), by Colin McCarty and Kate Ruttle (Hodder, 2012) is one of a number of stand-alone phonic assessment resources available for class teachers, specialist teachers and special educational needs coordinators (SENCOs).

Pera is matched to *Letters and Sounds* and the requirements of the Year 1 Phonics Screening Check. Pera uses real words and pseudo-words to assess phonic knowledge and the use of phonics for reading, plus reading accuracy and **comprehension**. There are two tests, each of 10 minutes, which are standardised over 3,500 pupils nationally.

Pera 1 assesses Phases 2–4 and is for use at the end of Reception and the first half of Year 1.

Pera 2 assesses Phases 3–5 and is for use in Year 1 and/or Year 2.

Diagnostic Test of Word Reading Processes

The Forum for Research into Language and Literacy's *Diagnostic Test of Word Reading Processes* (DTWRP) (GL Assessment, 2012) is a fully standardised test that assesses the children's ability to read words using both phonological and lexical-semantic processes. It provides diagnostic information to guide intervention.

The test is suitable for children aged 6–12 years. The test time is unlimited, but it should take no longer than 30 minutes.

Phonic assessment record (photocopiable)

Name   Dates

Grapheme	Recognise (can identify when asked to find or can say in response to grapheme)	Read (can read in a simple word)	Write (can write to spell a simple word)
s			
a			
t			
p			
i			
n			
m			
d			
g			
o			
c			
k			
ck			
e			
u			
r			
h			
b			
f, ff			
l, ll			
ss			
j			
v			
w			

Page 1 of 2

Grapheme	Recognise (can identify when asked to find or can say in response to grapheme)	Read (can read in a simple word)	Write (can write to spell a simple word)
x			
y			
z, zz			
qu			
ch			
sh			
th as in that			
th as in thin			
ng			
ai			
ee			
igh			
oa			
oo as in zoo			
oo as in book			
ar			
or			
ur			
ow			
oi			
ear			
air			
ure			
er			
ire			
nk*			

*Some schemes include this sound. © Rising Stars UK Ltd 2012. You may photocopy this page.

Different spellings of each phoneme

Name: Dates:

Known spelling of phoneme	New and different spellings of known phonemes	Recognise (can identify when asked to find or can say in response to grapheme)	Read (can read in a simple word)	Write (can write to spell a simple word)
ai	ay			
	a-e			
ee	ea			
	y			
	e-e			
igh	i-e			
	ie			
	i			
	y			
oa	ow			
	o-e			
	o			
oo	u-e			
	ue			
	ew			
or	oor			
	ore			
	aw			
	au			
air	are			
ur	ir			
	ur			
ow	ou			
oi	oy			

Page 1 of 2

Known spelling of phoneme	New and different spellings of known phonemes	Recognise (can identify when asked to find or can say in response to grapheme)	Read (can read in a simple word)	Write (can write to spell a simple word)
f, ff	ph			
l, ll	le			
m	mm			
	mb			
n	nn			
	kn			
r	rr			
	wr			
s	se			
	c			
	ce			
v	ve			
z, zz	s			
	se			
sh	ti as in **tion**			
	ci as in **cion**			
b	bb			
ck	ch			
d	dd			
g	gg			
j	g			
	dge			
p	pp			
t	tt			
w	wh			
ch	tch			
ch	ture			

CHAPTER 12 – CHOOSING RESOURCES

How to choose the best resources

As previously mentioned in this book, there are DfE criteria to help publishers to produce high-quality resources for **phonics** teaching and learning and to help teachers to make wise and fruitful purchasing decisions.

Published resources that appear on the DfE list of resources are acknowledged to be those that best support the teaching of high-quality systematic **synthetic phonics**. Publishers submit to a panel of experts who assess the resources against the list of criteria.

What is a mainstream core phonics teaching programme?

A mainstream core programme will meet all the criteria in the checklist and will by design have everything you need to deliver a full phonics teaching course. It may include elements that are considered to be supplementary. It will be expensive to buy and may 'lock' you in, but it will give you peace of mind and confidence. There may be core programmes for mainstream learners and core programmes for children who need to 'catch up'. For more about catch-up, refer to Chapter 10.

What is a supplementary resource?

A supplementary resource will meet most of the criteria in the checklist, but not all. It will be clear in its approach to systematic synthetic phonics and explicit about what it supports. It may be used alongside an existing core programme or with another supplementary programme or teacher-made resources.

What is a skill-specific resource?

A skill-specific resource is just that – it will offer opportunities to review, teach, practise or apply a specific skill. These resources are most usually game-related (e.g. a puzzle, collection of cards, computer program and so on).

What is equipment?

Equipment covers the additional physical resources that will help you as a teacher in your lesson delivery (e.g. write-on/wipe-off whiteboards, magnetic letters, bibs with pockets on the front for children to wear …).

Checklist for assessing resources

The following checklist is based on the DfE criteria for ensuring high-quality **phonics** work.

Name of resource	
Mainstream core phonics teaching programme? All boxes should be ticked. **Supplementary resource?** Most boxes should be ticked. **Skill-specific resource?** Some boxes should be ticked. **Equipment?** Some boxes should be ticked.	
Does the resource:	**Tick to confirm**
Offer a coherent and consistent approach and incremental teaching sequence throughout the programme?	
Enable you to review, check and assess the children's progress?	
Present systematic, synthetic phonic work as the main approach to **decoding** print, i.e. a phonics 'first and fast' approach?	
Enable the children to start learning phonic knowledge and skills using a systematic, synthetic programme by the age of 5?	
Expect the children to be fluent readers with secure word recognition skills by the end of Key Stage 1?	
Support you to deliver a discrete, daily phonic lesson progressing from simple to more complex phonic knowledge and skills and covering the major **grapheme–phoneme** correspondences?	
Demonstrate or explicitly recommend that phonemes should be blended, in order, from left to right, 'all through the word' for reading?	
Demonstrate or explicitly recommend how words can be segmented into phonemes for spelling and that this is the reverse of **blending** phonemes to read words?	
Promote that children apply phonic knowledge and skills as their *first* approach to reading and spelling even if a word is not completely phonically regular?	
Promote that children are taught high-frequency and **tricky words**?	
Use a multi-sensory approach so that children learn from a mix of visual, auditory and kinaesthetic activities which are designed to nurture and secure essential phonic knowledge and skills?	

Checklist for hands-on resources

Use this checklist to audit your resources and to identify resource gaps.

Resource	Practice for ...	Yes/No or notes
Soft toy/puppet	**Sound-talk** (e.g. Reading Writing Inc. Fred the Frog); word building, spelling (e.g. Cheeky Chimps)	
Flashcards: graphemes	Oral letter–sound recognition	
Flashcards: picture cards of phonemes	Oral letter–sound recognition	
Picture scene word mats	Vocabulary, spelling	
Audio phonemes tiles	Listening, saying the sounds (e.g. Jolly Phonics with TTS)	
Phonic bibs and pockets	Word building, blending and **segmenting** (e.g. Yellow Door)	
Phonic phoneme fans: • for phases • for **high-frequency words**	Blending and segmenting	
High-frequency word posters	Classroom reminders	
Flashcards: high-frequency words	Blending, word recognition	
Brick kit or phonic cubes for graphemes	Word building, spelling	
Giant and/or small pocket dice	Blending and segmenting games	
High-frequency and tricky words: balls or bean bags	Blending and word recognition	
Phonemes: balls or bean bags	Blending and word recognition	
Ping-pong balls	Grapheme recognition, spelling (e.g. TTS)	
Letter tiles: • interconnecting • magnetic • on IWB	Blending and segmenting at word level or phrase, sentence level practice (e.g. Poly-phonics Polydron, 2Simple Phonic)	
Letter flip books	Blending and segmenting	
Sentence strips	Blending and segmenting of phrases, sentences, questions	
Phoneme frames	Segmenting, writing	
Write-on/wipe-off whiteboards	Letter formation, spelling	
Grid board cards (large display board for building words)	Blending and segmenting	
Alternative grapheme displays	Spelling choices, writing (e.g. Best Bet Train Cards – Lesley Clarke)	
Self-checking games	Blending and segmenting (e.g. Smart Learning Spelling, Accelerator Spelling)	
Picture–word matching games	Reading words, phrases, sentences	
Alternative spelling puzzles	Spelling (e.g. Smart Kids)	
Phoneme spotters	Phoneme recognition (e.g. Smart Kids)	
Wooden split **digraph** pieces	Spelling (e.g. TTS)	

CHAPTER 13 GAMES TO GO

Phonics lessons work best when the teaching and resources meet the specified DfE criteria, but in the end it's the teacher or adult engaging with the children who makes the critical difference. Lessons that are exciting, fun, creative, collaborative and interactive will almost certainly engage children in their learning.

So how can we best deliver an engaging lesson?

Use the resources you've already purchased

⭐ Core programmes will be packed with resources to use and activity ideas to make, so get the most from them.

⭐ Adapt resources you have purchased but have shortcomings; get the children to help you with ideas!

Use online resources (with care)

⭐ Search online for some great ideas and templates, but always assess them carefully and adapt them for your own needs. Check out 'Mr Thorne does Phonics' which can be found on the *Times Educational Supplement* website www.tes.co.uk for some fun games based on the old favourites such as 'Bingo', 'Family Fortunes' and 'Connect Four', and some new ones too such as 'Word Wallpaper' and 'Clever Quiz'.

A phonics game from www.educationcity.com.

⭐ Search for game-based learning sites, e.g. www.educationcity.com.

Use props and a great deal of imagination

⭐ If you have a puppet or even a sock that could become a puppet – then use it to pretend that it cannot get phonics right – the children will love to correct it or tell it what to do. They also like to have a go at controlling the puppet.

⭐ If you have a small soft ball or bean bag, use it for a circle time phonics game, e.g. when you catch it you have to say a word that features a specific sound, or you have to read a word from the board, spell a word from a picture on the board, etc.

Use a sock puppet for fun games.

Use a stopwatch or egg timer, or put the children into teams, to energise their efforts and enhance the pace of the lesson.

Make your own resources

Remember the old games are often the best – just rejig them to ensure that they are focused on your learning objective. For example:

 play 'I Spy', but use letter sounds, not names

 play 'Bingo' with letter sounds or **sound-talk**, not numbers

 play 'Simon Says' using sound-talk, not words.

These are just a few ideas – use your imagination! Keep a file of these games so that when you forget a particular game you can pull it out and use it with fresh energy. Or when you read about a new game you can store it for when the time is right.

Photocopiable resources

On the following pages you'll find a few useful photocopiable resources:

 Long **vowel** phoneme picture cards   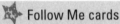 Follow Me cards

 High-frequency word cards – first 100

Any of these may be copied as personal sets of **flashcards** or copied in duplicates and cut up to play 'Snap', or used in conjunction with a baseboard to play 'Bingo' or other similar games.

Further photocopiable resources include:

 Phoneme frames for words with two, three, four, five and six phonemes for children to practise spelling; in pairs, in teams or even against the clock.

> Write the word. Cut it up.
> Ask a friend to rebuild it.

A template for a 'Follow Me' game – a game which involves creating a chain reaction. This can be played simply using letters and sounds or for more complex teaching points such as practising alternative spellings of a phoneme.

Follow Me game

'Follow Me' game to practise
grapheme–phoneme recognition

(The children say the letter sound.)

Start

I have **g**.
Who has **i**?

•

I have **i**.
Who has **d**?

•

I have **d**.
Who has **sh**?

Etc.

'Follow Me' game to practise
different spellings of /ee/

Start

I have **bean**.
Who has **bee**?

•

I have **bee.**
Who has **jeans**?

•

I have **jeans**.
Who has **swede**?

Etc.

Outdoor phonics? Yes, really!

Many training programmes now include practical ideas for phonics teaching outside in big and small spaces. Use footballs, nets, cones or bean bags to inspire those children who respond better to physical activities than to sitting inactively in a classroom.

TOP TIP ✓

Try a phonic treasure hunt.

Print and laminate **graphemes** or words, and hide them outside.

As the children find them they tick the pictures off a list.

First to find them all is the winner!

Phonics Outdoor Signs from TTS Group.

Outdoor High-Frequency Words from TTS Group.

Phoneme frames

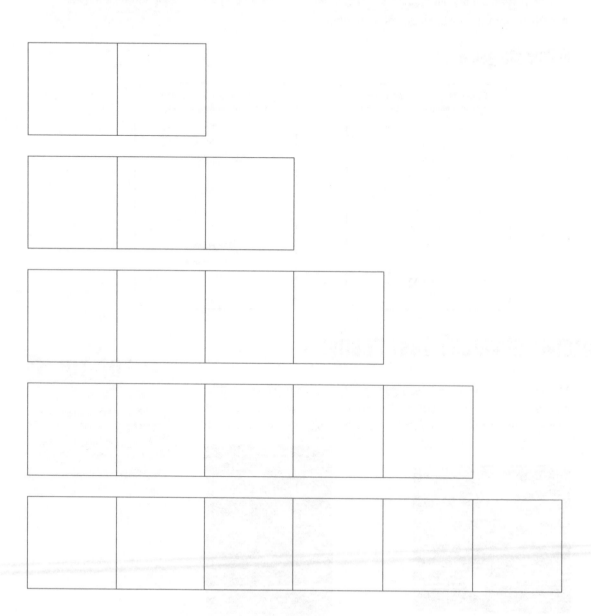

Long Vowel Phoneme Picture Cards

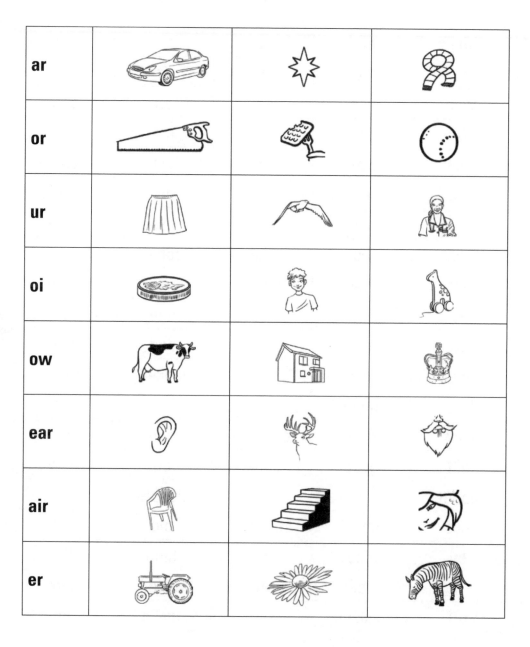

ar			
or			
ur			
oi			
ow			
ear			
air			
er			

High-Frequency Word Cards – First 100

the	and	a	to	said
in	he	I	of	it
was	you	they	on	she
is	for	at	his	but
that	with	all	we	can
are	up	had	my	her
what	there	out	this	have
went	be	like	some	so
not	then	were	go	little
as	no	mum	one	them
do	me	down	dad	big
when	it's	see	looked	very
look	don't	will	into	come
back	from	children	him	Mr
get	just	came	oh	now
about	got	their	people	your
put	could	house	old	too
by	day	made	time	I'm
if	help	Mrs	called	here
off	asked	saw	make	an

Follow Me cards

START I have Who has	I have Who has	I have Who has	I have Who has	I have Who has	I have Who has
I have Who has	I have Who has	I have Who has	I have Who has	I have Who has	I have Who has
I have Who has	I have Who has	I have Who has	I have Who has	I have Who has	I have Who has
I have Who has	I have Who has	I have Who has	I have Who has	I have Who has	I have Who has
I have Who has	I have Who has	I have Who has	I have Who has	I have Who has	I have Who has
I have Who has	I have Who has	I have Who has	I have Who has	I have Who has	I have **End**

GLOSSARY AND KEY

Glossary

Alphabetic code This is the code that explains the relationship between the sounds of speech and the written letter(s) of the alphabet and how these match those sounds.

Blending To say the individual sounds that make up a word and blend them together to hear the whole word for reading, e.g. **c-a-t** becomes **cat**. We say you blend to read and segment (see below) to spell.

Comprehension The understanding of a text; at its simplest this may be an understanding of what the text makes explicit, e.g. the story is about a giant and, at its most sophisticated, it is an understanding of what lies beneath a text, e.g. the experience, voice, etc. Comprehension flourishes when **decoding** is secure.

Consonant Every letter in the English alphabet that is not a **vowel**.

Decodable (books or text) Books or text which have been specifically written, using a cumulative structured introduction of **phonics**, so that children can practise their developing reading skills.

Decoding To read a word by saying the sounds then joining, or **blending**, those sounds together to form the word.

Digraphs Two letters that represent one sound, e.g. a **consonant** digraph is **ch** and a **vowel** digraph is **ai**.

Dyslexia Dyslexia is a specific learning difficulty which mainly affects the development of literacy- and language-related skills. For further information visit www.bdadyslexia.org.uk.

Flashcards Cards to use in games to help the children practise recognising, at speed, a letter, group of letters, words and/or pictures.

Graphemes A written letter or group of letters that represent a sound, e.g. the sound /k/ can be represented by the graphemes **c** in **clap**, **k** in **yak**, **ck** in **tick**, **ch** in **Christmas** and so on.

High-frequency words These are the words that occur most commonly in the English language. Some are 'decodable' such as **him**, **like** or **up** (see **decoding**) whilst others are 'tricky' like **the**, **they** and **people** (see **tricky words**).

Mnemonics Memory joggers such as a rhyme, a phrase or a shape. An example is showing a letter **m** drawn over the shape of a mountain to help the children to associate the picture with the letter and sound **m**, but this is really only useful in the early stages.

Phonemic awareness A narrower term than **phonological awareness** (see below) relating to being able to specifically identify and manipulate **phonemes** of spoken words.

Phonics A method of teaching children to read and write the English language. It teaches children that the sounds of English are represented by letters or groups of letters (see also **synthetic phonics**).

Phonemes The smallest unit of sound in a word represented by letters or groups of letter, e.g. the sound /k/ can be represented by the letters **c**, **k**, **ck** and **ch**.

Phonological awareness A broad term relating to being able to identify and manipulate the sounds of spoken language, e.g. rhyme, syllables, words and even **phonemes**.

Segmenting To write or spell a word by listening for the sounds in the word and deciding which letters represent those sounds. We say you blend to read and segment to spell.

Sight-words Words you need to learn by sight because they cannot be easily sounded out (see also **tricky words**).

Sound-talk To say the individual sounds that make up a word. It sometimes takes on different names, e.g. Robot Talk.

Sounding out To say the individual sounds that make up a word, as in **sound-talk**.

Synthesising sounds Blending or merging the sounds in a word together in speech so you can read the word.

Synthetic phonics Synthetic phonics is a way of teaching the **alphabetic code** so children can learn to read and spell. The children are taught to read letters or groups of letters by saying the sound(s) they represent – so, they are taught that the letter **s** sounds like **ssss** … when we say it. The children can then start to read words by **blending** (**synthesising**) the sounds together to make a word.

Tricky words Common words that are difficult to decode because some of the letters don't make the sounds you would expect, like **the** or **said** (see also **high-frequency words**).

Vowels The letters **a**, **e**, **i**, **o**, **u** in the English alphabet.

Key

CV consonant–vowel **to**, **but**, **say**

VC vowel–consonant **on**, **but**, **oil**

VCC vowel–consonant–consonant **act**, **ask**, **imp**

CVC consonant–vowel–consonant **cat**, **head**, **make**

CCVC consonant–consonant–vowel–consonant **trim**, **stove**, **bread**, **thrush**

CVCC consonant–vowel–consonant–consonant **bank**, **joust**

CCVCC consonant–consonant–vowel–consonant–consonant **clump**, **clowns**, **shrink**

CCCV consonant–consonant–consonant –vowel **spree**

CCCVC consonant–consonant– consonant–vowel–consonant **strap**, **scrape**

CCCVCC consonant–consonant–consonant–vowel–consonant–consonant **strict**